Defense Strategy
For Women
<u>Be Your Own Risk Manager!</u>

by David R. Locke & Kent L. Maurer

SALTBOX PRESS
SPRING ARBOR, MICHIGAN

Dedication

To the four women in my life: My mother, Lillian; my
wife, Laura; and my children, Angela and Jennifer.
-- Kent L. Maurer

To my wife, Carol; my daughter, Michelle; and my son
David, for their love and support.
-- David R. Locke

Published in Spring Arbor, Michigan by Saltbox Press.
Distributed by *Defensive Strategy for Women,* P.O. Box
1901, Jackson, Michigan 49204

Printed in the United States of America
September, 1991
ISBN: 1-878559-02-8

Contents

Acknowledgements

The authors would like to thank the following people for their support and contributions to this book:

To the staff at Aware Inc., a shelter for domestic violence and sexual assault counseling, for review of the chapter on acquaintance assault. To Robert L. Johnson for his support and encouragement of this book and its predecessor, *Defensive Tactics for Women.* To Anthony Raduazo for his review of legal portions of this book. To Dan Runyon for his editing and publishing skills. To Cindy Lyons for illustrating the book. To Renee Runyon for proofreading. To Lewis Okun for his review of the book. A special thank you to Ann Zimmerman for her insight into the chapter about senior citizens. And to the 1500 women who have participated in our seminars and presentations about rape prevention and have contributed heavily to this work.

Introduction

This book teaches about crime awareness, particularly crimes against women. Our purpose is to give you the knowledge, insight, and confidence you need to minimize the occasion of becoming a crime victim, and to be prepared in advance for the unexpected.

Most people reading books about self-defense want to read exciting and detailed stories about successful defenses. They hope to learn some sure-fire techniques to immobilize an attacker.

This book outlines strategies that have worked for women to avoid or escape a rape attack. However, we offer these strategies with caution. No strategy can work in every situation. A constant sense of reality must temper any predictions of success of any crime prevention technique. There are no shortcuts to self-protection and crime prevention.

The theme of this book is in the title, *Defense Strategy for Women.* *Strategy* refers to a pattern of decisions you make over a long time period, and directed toward a particular goal. Private corporations, the military, sporting events, and people working in many other arenas have a strategy. Their strategy is always geared to survival and growth. In the same way, *defense strategy* refers to a pattern of planned decisions over a long time period, and directed toward the personal goal of self-protection. That is, self-protection is not left to chance.

The subtitle *Be Your Own Risk Manager,* completes the equation. A *manager* is one who recognizes and directs the resources of an organization. *Risks* are events with potentially negative consequences. You can manage personal risks in the same way, by directing your resources in a way that reduces or removes the risk.

This is not a motivational book that promises to make you a skilled fighting machine. And we cannot guarantee that you will not become a victim of a criminal act. However, following the strategies we outline can minimize your vulnerability to crime. Becoming a risk manager is a pro-active approach that helps you understand your fear of crime and implement a preventive strategy to combat crime.

1. Prevention:
First Step To Self-Defense

Crime prevention is the anticipation, recognition and appraisal of a crime risk and the

*initiation of actions to remove
or reduce it.*[1]

This quotation defines crime prevention and serves as the working framework for law enforcement crime prevention programs in England, the United States and other nations.

What Is Crime Prevention?

Crime prevention is an action plan for individuals, neighborhood groups and organizations to work with local law enforcement agencies to minimize the potential of becoming a crime victim. Embedded solidly in the crime prevention philosophy is the necessity for crime awareness training and active participation in programs like "neighborhood watch," "operation identification," "rape prevention," etc.

Crime prevention is an attitude where people realize that law enforcement alone cannot reduce crime. This attitude calls for us to change old habits (not always easy to do) regarding how we protect property, family members and ourselves from becoming victims of crime.

Crime prevention requires both participation and involvement. Adults normally resist making changes, such as breaking old habits, because it is uncomfortable to do so at first. Motivation to change old habits begins when the consequences of not changing are perceived to be too costly.

Many people still resist using vehicle restraint systems. They have not installed smoke detectors. They continue to ignore that regular exercise and proper nutrition can be beneficial. They resist making changes even though the best information tells us that we really should do these

---

[1]A.A. Kingsbury, *Introduction to Security and Crime Prevention Survey* (Springfield, IL: Charles C. Thomas, Publisher, 1973), p. 6.

things for our well-being. The reasons to ignore sound advice are many and includes the rationalization that "crime always happens to the other person, not to me."

The following story illustrates how using crime prevention techniques can minimize losses when victimized:

A Home Burglary

Bill and Diane entered their driveway one afternoon. Their two children were in school. They entered the house from the garage and discovered their home had been violated by thieves. The master bedroom was in a shambles with the mattress pulled from the bed, dresser drawers pulled out, and jewelry boxes thrown to the floor.

Shocked and angered, Bill and Diane still remembered not to unnecessarily touch any of the items before a police officer could search for evidence. While waiting for police officials to arrive, Bill and Diane realized that the family losses in this crime were minimal, thanks to the crime prevention strategies they practiced. For example:

1. Important papers and antique jewelry were stored in a safety deposit box.
2. All family valuables were listed on a home inventory sheet, which was now available for accurate reporting to the police.
3. No large amounts of cash were kept in the home.
4. Valuables were not stored in the bedroom or kitchen cupboards, the most common place for crooks to search first for valuables.

The monetary loss to Bill and Diane was minimal, but the psychological impact on their family could have been significant if handled improperly. Bill and Diane had read extensively about crime prevention. They realized a home burglary means a psychological loss, for the home is a private place and provides a sense of family security. This security had been violated by strangers.

Bill and Diane decided to discuss the incident with

their children, but only after restoring the home to its usual neat appearance (after the police investigation and before the children arrived home).

Bill and Diane reappraised their crime prevention strategies in light of this incident and decided to improve home security by installing new deadbolt locks in the entrance doors and to remain vigilant in their crime prevention habits.

Preventive Habits

Habits are behaviors we have developed over a period of time and include both positive and negative behaviors. Some of our habits have been reinforced for many years and are not easy to break without a strong desire or incentive to do so. How many have either tried to stop smoking or start a regular exercise program?

Are you prevention oriented? Do you routinely practice habits that enhance the safety of you and your family? To find out, review the following questions:

1. Do you routinely use vehicle seat belts?
2. Have you installed smoke detectors in your home?
3. Are you involved in a routine personal fitness program?
4. Do you lock your house at night or when it is unoccupied?
5. Do you practice safety policies in the workplace, such as wearing safety glasses and other protective devices?
6. Have you taken inventory of the valuables in your home?

These questions do not constitute an empirical study, and scientific conclusions cannot be drawn from your answers. We offer them to stimulate your thinking about matters of safety and crime prevention. If your answer to the majority of these questions is "yes," you should easily be able to learn and practice crime prevention habits. If your answer is "no," you may find it more difficult to routinely practice crime prevention strategies.

Crime prevention requires much effort on the part of all members of society. Practicing crime prevention "habits" requires special effort and motivation to replace the old habits. It is your choice.

Privacy: A Foe to Prevention

As active crime prevention practitioners, we have learned that American society has rapidly become fast-paced and one which treasures individual privacy. We are also a transient people. Many of the older neighborhoods are occupied by short-term residents. In many neighborhoods we are seeing a shift from families knowing one another to "rows of houses" occupied by strangers who live in isolation from each other.

Law enforcement crime prevention specialists address the issue of *apathy* to community members in crime awareness training sessions. Ironically, many Americans are still indifferent and do not practice sound crime prevention strategies at home, while shopping, in the car, or on vacation. To see if you fit this category, ask yourself the following questions:

1. I will/will not report a suspicious person or vehicle to the police department.
2. I will/will not make an inventory of all valuables in my home to include brand names, model, serial number and description.
3. I will/will not invest this year to improve the security of my home.
4. I will/will not inquire at my local police or sheriff's department about involvement in crime prevention programs.
5. I have/have not invested more money in recreational vehicles and equipment than in home security

hardware, such as locks, lighting, alarms, etc.

6.   I believe/do not believe it is easier to accept insurance reimbursement for stolen property than to invest in and practice crime prevention recommendations.

A negative answer to all of these questions is not necessarily a sign of apathy. But we do know that too many people, in their hurried, private lives, assume that law enforcement is solely responsible for preventing crime. The reality is that there probably won't be an officer nearby when you need one.

It is unfortunate that today many homes cannot be left without the owner fearing that he or she will be burglarized, and it is not fair that many people of all ages are afraid of being attacked while out in the community. Yet this is a fact of life today.

Law enforcement officials search constantly for new methods to make communities safe and to reduce crime occurrences. You as a citizen can also reduce crime by practicing realistic crime prevention habits, participating in neighborhood watch programs, and learning about crime prevention in a spirit of cooperation with local law enforcement agencies. Law enforcement cannot do the job alone.

Crime Prevention: Become Your Own Risk Manager

As a result of experiencing both internal and external losses, private businesses have realized the need to study company "risks" in a pro-active approach. The sophisticated security programs that resulted now greatly reduce company losses due to thefts, accidents and fire. The title "Loss Prevention Manager" or "Risk Manager" is given to the men and women responsible for administering such loss prevention programs.

Your can take a similar pro-active approach by becoming a "personal risk manager." As a risk manager you become concerned for the security and welfare of a much smaller unit than if for a company. Your primary concern is yourself, your family, significant others, or your neighborhood.

Here are three factors to keep in mind when thinking about risk: how *vulnerable* are you, how *probable* is the crime, and how *critical* would the result be?[2]

1. Vulnerability: In our definition of crime prevention we suggested that you evaluate and appraise crime risks in your personal life:

- Are you involved in neighborhood watch?
- Have you inquired of your police department for a possible free home crime prevention inspection?
- Have you considered installation of a CB radio or cellular phone for your vehicle in case of emergencies?
- Are you careful about giving personal information over the telephone, or when a stranger knocks at your door?

(Further discussion of preventive strategies will be explored in chapter 5.)

2. Probability: Most people prefer not to spend much time thinking about this. However, failure to recognize the probability of becoming a crime victim could be a costly mistake. The following Federal Bureau of Investigation (FBI) national averages of recent years reveal:[3]
1. One violent crime every 20 seconds.
2. One property crime every 3 seconds.

---

[2]Based on Karen Hess and Henry Wrobleski, *Introduction to Private Security* (St. Paul, MN: West Publishing, 1982), p. 59.

[3]Federal Bureau of Investigation *Uniform Crime Reports, 1986 to 1989.*

3. One forcible rape every 6 minutes.
4. One murder every 25 minutes.
5. One aggravated assault every 36 seconds.
6. One burglary every 10 seconds.

These statistics are not being presented to foster paranoia, but to focus on reality. Crime prevention programs sponsored by law enforcement agencies and private business for their employees attempt to deliver this message: You can no longer ignore the possibility of becoming a crime victim.

3. Criticality: In the private security field, criticality refers to the cost of loss. There is an obvious parallel when examining minimum and maximum consequences when considering the cost of becoming a crime victim. You should ask yourself "What is the worst-case scenario for me in this situation?" or "What is the best-case scenario for me in this situation?"

The grievous error is to make the same mistake as private businesses did for many years by not asking these questions or conducting the examination at all.

The acronym PREVENT explains the principles of prevention and provides a foundation for building your crime prevention strategy:

P Plan and Prepare. Planning requires thinking ahead and considering the potential of physical confrontation in crime situations, such as becoming a purse snatching victim or sexual assault victim. To plan for such occurrences, practice "what if" scenarios in your mind, or discuss the situation with friends and family.

Police officers use "what if" scenario-based training in both recruit academies and in the field training experience. For example, the training officer might say to a recruit: "What if we received a dispatch that an armed robbery is in progress at the XYZ party store? What route will you take to the store? What will you do once you arrive?"

An example of "what if" scenario-based thinking for you might be this: What if I am confronted in the parking lot by a mugger? What will I do? What avenues of possible escape exist? What potential weapons are at my disposal? What will I say? Thinking through imagined emergency situations may provide you with an effective course of action when facing a similar situation in reality.

The worst scenario is when you fall victim of a confrontation with no forethought or defense plan and allow fear and panic responses to completely dictate your reactions.

Of course, there are NO GUARANTEES with this (or with any) strategy. The goal of practicing the "what if" exercise is to have a plan should you face a threatening situation, instead of being caught completely off-guard, surprised and unknowing.

R *Recognize Your Attitude* of "It can't happen to me." This is unrealistic and promotes an unprepared state. Getting involved in community crime prevention programs is a positive step toward reducing crime in your community. YOU are primarily responsible for properly securing your home and property. It is YOUR responsibility to daily practice preventive techniques. We encourage people to seriously consider contacting their local law enforcement agencies and inquire about crime prevention programs. After all, you pay for these programs through tax dollars.

E *Evaluate and Appraise* the crime risks in your home and personal practices. YOU know, and can appraise the security weaknesses in your home better than anyone. YOU know, and can appraise your personal habits and risks better than anyone.

A crime risk is defined as "an opportunity for crime" to occur. Examples include inadequate door locks, unlocked doors, poor outdoor lighting, walking alone at night, picking up a hitchhiker, and so on. An important step in minimizing a crime risk is to be the one to initiate action to remove or reduce the risk.

Leaving the house unlocked provides an opportunity for easy access by a thief. The solution is simple, but requires changing your habits and initiating action by locking the doors and windows. While crime prevention specialists can recommend avoidance strategies and techniques, it is your responsibility to act on the recommendations.

Finally, the process of evaluation involves making *choices* and establishing *priorities.* Many people invest hundreds or even thousands of dollars on recreation, yet they think investing $500 on improving home security is not important.

V Victims are not always at the mercy of their attackers. Everyone is a victim of crime, either directly or indirectly. We are the victims of crime *directly* if it is our house that is broken into, or our purse that is stolen. We are the victims of crime *indirectly* through added costs of retail merchandise (because of thefts), increased insurance costs, and the costs for criminal justice services.

Planning and practicing alternative strategies can impact the outcome in many assaultive crimes. In Chapter 7 we will explore examples of alternatives that might prevent a person from becoming a victim. Examining alternatives from the three categories of physical, non-physical and weapon may be a positive step toward not becoming a victim at all.

E Educate yourself about crime prevention

techniques through law enforcement-sponsored crime prevention programs. Many private businesses have developed excellent crime prevention programs and offer printed materials for employees and their families. Another good source for crime prevention books and articles is a local college or public library. The authors feel it is a parental responsibility to educate children about relevant crime prevention matters. We hope this text is just one of many sources you will use for educational growth about crime prevention issues.

N Negative Thinking can affect your attitudes about survival. To illustrate, we have stressed that we cannot guarantee anyone reading this book that he or she will never become a victim of crime. A negative thinking person is likely to say, "There is no sense wasting my time reading this book. There is nothing I can do if someone chooses me as a victim."

We recommend a more realistic attitude. By studying a variety of preventive strategies and gaining a clear picture of the crime problems in your community, a survival attitude can be developed that says, "I will survive this situation." This attitude fosters pre-planning and serious consideration of what constitutes survival.

T Training and Practice are the keys to mastering the techniques and concepts necessary to survive an assault confrontation. As boring as it might sound, constant repetition is the only route to skill proficiency.

We are not referring merely to new skill acquisition such as self-defense techniques, but also to the daily repetition of crime prevention techniques such as locking the house whenever you leave. The goal is to develop prevention techniques that you practice without stopping to think about them. They become automatic and offer increased chances of not becoming a crime victim.

Old habits are difficult to break, but once the new habits are mastered, little energy is required to maintain them. Remember how difficult it was at first to remember to buckle-up? But now it has become as natural as closing the car door. And good defensive drivers are ever vigilant of the road and the actions of other drivers. Countless accidents have been avoided because of alert defensive actions by one of the drivers. In the same way, countless crimes are prevented because of crime prevention steps taken by many people.

The remainder of this book provides recommendations, strategies, techniques and skills to become better prepared for crime prevention to minimize your crime vulnerability.

2. Fear
And Perception Of Danger

A person's immediate reaction in a threatening situation is not always predictable. Some people freeze with fear and become immobile. Others feel a burst of adrenaline and find

*strength they never knew they
had. Still others act very calmly
and clearly at the time, but
crumble in a flood of emotional
fear and tears several days
later. People don't always
react the way they imagine
they would when actually
confronted with an assault.*[1]

Fear

Conflict is based on emotion. Two of the emotions
that normally accompany conflict are anger and fear --
legitimate feelings and normal responses for human beings
in a crisis.

One of the strongest fears is the "fear of the
unknown." Becoming informed about an actual problem
instead of reacting to a perceived problem means better
preparation and increased opportunities for success. Brian's
story illustrates what we mean:

Brian's Story

Brian had been unable to sleep for three nights
running -- the exact length of time since his family moved
to the "new" old house. Mom and Dad fell in love with the
1930's Victorian home and moved across town to accept
the challenge of renovating the slightly neglected structure.

The terror was about to begin again. As darkness
creeped toward his room, Brian hid his six-year-old frame
between the sheets of his bed and ducked his head under
the pillow.

Mom and Dad had said the noises Brian heard at
night were from the steam heat, the settling timbers, and

---

[1]Shirley Pettifer and Janet Torge, *A Book About Sexual
Assault* (Montreal Press Inc., 1987), p. 10.

the wind weaving through exterior spaces. However, it seemed to Brian that ghosts were omnipresent each night.

Brian was prepared for battle. He had carefully locked the bedroom door, then propped a chair under the door handle from the inside. His slingshot was loaded and would be held tightly in his hand throughout the night. His covers were pulled tightly around his shoulders, and only his nose could be seen from beneath the pillow.

In time, Brian will accept the truth about the haunting noises. For now he is convinced that it is necessary to invest his efforts in combating a perceived problem by attacking the symptoms and not the causes. His reaction is based on fear and emotion, not on facts.

Fear is prevalent in our society. *The Figgie Report on Fear of Crime* reveals that four out of ten Americans are very much afraid they will become victims of violent crimes such as murder, rape, robbery, or assault. Four out of ten Americans also feel unsafe in their homes, neighborhoods, business districts and shopping centers.[2]

The Figgie Report identified two types of fear related to crime. *Concrete Fear* is the fear of becoming the victim of a specific violent crime. *Formless Fear* is a non-specific fear about safety in one's home, neighborhood and larger community.[3]

Concrete fear permits factual discussion to determine if it is well-placed fear. A review of crime data and discussions with neighbors or police officers will reveal the actual incidence of a particular crime. *Formless* fear is not so easy to alleviate or confirm. Formless fear may be based on attitudes, perceptions, beliefs and value systems

---

[2]*The Figgie Report on Fear of Crime: America Afraid Part I, The General Public* (Research & Forecasts, Inc., 1980), pp. 14-15.

[3]Ibid., p. 29.

acquired since childhood which comprise our frame of reference.

Frame of Reference

Your frame of reference is the perspective from which you view people and events, and how you relate and communicate with them. The primary components of your frame of reference are your values, beliefs and attitudes. Understanding how values, beliefs and attitudes affect perceptions is important to students of crime prevention and self-defense.

Dr. Tom Muldary summarizes the concepts of values, beliefs and attitudes:

> Values, as notions about the way things 'should be' are different from beliefs, which are convictions about the way things 'are'. Beliefs consist of facts, general knowledge, and assumptions acquired through our interactions with the environment and other people. Beliefs and values are different from one another and still different from attitudes... They are also learned, relatively enduring, and can be changed... because attitudes 'predispose' us to react in specific ways towards those with whom we interact....[4]

Values are the things people consider to be right or wrong, important or unimportant. Values are personal measures that judge the worth or importance of something in the environment. *Beliefs* are the mental acceptance of truth or actuality, something a person accepts as being true or factual. Beliefs are conviction, personal notions, opinions and sentiments. Leonard Doob describes beliefs as:

---

[4]Dr. Thomas W. Muldary, *Interpersonal Relations for Health Professionals* (Eastern Michigan University, MacMillan Publishing Co.), p. 199.

...a stereotype ideology or myth, whether valid or not... which is supported by what its possessor considers to be relevant, valid knowledge. Many beliefs, whether buttressed with knowledge or not, cannot be verbalized easily.[5]

Our understanding of *belief* is helped by this observation from Edward Bettinghaus and Michael Cody:

To express the relationships we see between two or more events or people or the relationships between events and characteristics of those events. Thus, I can express... a belief by saying 'I believe Ford cars are very durable....' Although we cannot directly observe... a belief, we can find out about it. This is done by making inferences from the observable behavior of an individual to what we think the person's internal state might be. One man hits another in a bar, and we infer that negative feelings are being displayed.[6]

Attitudes are a frame of mind affecting one's thoughts or behavior. An attitude can be a general cast of mind with regard to something, or a personal predisposition to feel a certain way about something. In the book *Interpersonal Relations for Health Professionals,* Dr. Tom Muldary describes an attitude as, "a relatively stable effective predisposition to respond in a particular way towards a person, object, or issue." Muldary goes on to say that attitudes tend to endure over time, remaining

---

[5]Leonard W. Doob, *Personality, Power and Authority: A View from the Behavioral Sciences* (Greenwood Press), pp. 73-74.

[6]Edward Bettinghaus and Michael J. Cody, *Persuasive Communication* (Holt Reinhart and Winston, 1987), pp. 8-9.

basically the same without significant change, and involve an emotional readiness to act in particular ways.[7]

Thus, values, beliefs and attitudes provide a frame of reference dictating how we interpret events, people and objects, and dictate how other people perceive us. If our frame of reference is based upon wrongly interpreted information, our false perceptions may result in unneeded investments of time, energy or money.

Consider the example of Mary. She is working in the kitchen when she feels water dripping on her head. After a brief inspection she determines that the water is dripping from the ceiling. Several phone calls and a week later Mary has arranged for a new roof to be installed on her house.

Mary is again working in the kitchen and again feels water dripping on her head. Her first impulse is to sue the roofing company. Her second impulse is to explore the problem more carefully. A few moments in the attic reveal that a water pipe routed through the ceiling is the source of the dripping water.

Myths About Crime and Sexual Assault

Many myths and misinformation exist about crime and sexual assault, resulting in faulty frames of reference. A myth is based on beliefs and attitudes, rather than upon fact and hard evidence. A myth is a body of traditional beliefs and notions accumulated about a particular subject. A myth is fiction and has no proven factual basis. Here are a few of the myths about sexual assault and crime:

1. *Myth:* Most sexual assaults of "rapes" are committed by an assailant who is unknown to the victim.
   Fact: The vast majority of sexual assaults are committed by a person who is acquainted with,

---

[7]Opcit., p. 209.

related to, or a member of the same household as the victim. "If you are a woman, your risk of being raped by someone you know is four times greater than your risk of being raped by a stranger."[8] The people who are sexually assaulted by a person they know are no less victims than those assaulted by strangers. However, your preparation for the actual (as opposed to the perceived) sexual assault problem may differ.

2. **Myth:** Crime is something that happens to other people. My chances of becoming a victim of crime are remote at best.
Fact: The chances of the ordinary person becoming a victim of crime are relatively high. A four-year average of crime statistics reveals that somewhere in the United States a murder occurs every 25 minutes, a forcible rape occurs every 6 minutes, a robbery occurs every 58 seconds, an aggravated assault occurs every 36 seconds, a burglary occurs every 10 seconds, a theft occurs every 4 seconds, and a car is stolen every 23 seconds.[9]

3. **Myth:** It is not possible to rape a non-consenting woman.
Fact: A non-consenting woman is raped every 6 minutes somewhere in the U.S. This myth ignores the factors of male and female anatomy. The myth also ignores the traditional socialization differences between men and women which imparts assertive, sometimes aggressive expectations upon the male.

---

[8]Robin Warshaw, *I Never Called It Rape* (Harper and Row, 1988), p. 11.

[9]*Uniform Crime Reports*, Federal Bureau of Investigation, 1986 through 1989.

The myth also ignores the size and strength differences between men and women in general.

This myth ignores the ability of an attacker to knock out a victim by the use of physical force, drugs, or alcohol, or to attack a sleeping victim and to use weapons or physical superiority to coerce obedience.

4. **Myth:** The only women who get raped are those who are "loose" and probably have "asked for it" anyway.

Fact: Most rape victims are members of the same household, related to, or acquainted with the attacker. This refutes the stereotypical view of the "loose" woman standing on the street corner and being raped. "Any female may become a victim of rape. Factors such as extreme youth, advanced age, physical homeliness and virginal life-style do not provide a foolproof deterrent or render a woman impervious to sexual assault."[10]

5. **Myth:** If I am the victim of a rape it will do no good to report it to the police because they will not believe me and I will be the one on trial.

Fact: Many states have laws which prevent the victim from being placed in the position of being on trial. In many states the victim cannot be asked by the police to submit to a lie detector test to "prove" that she is telling the truth. Police agencies have become more enlightened in the past 15 years as to the trauma of rape and steps necessary to offer empathetic investigative techniques. Most communities offer rape counseling and support

---

[10]Susan Brownmiller, *Against Our Will* (Bantam Books, 1986), p. 388.

services for victims of rape or assault. In most instances, the victim's prior sexual activity is not relevant to the case and cannot be entered into trial testimony.

These myths affect our frame of reference and fear of crime problems and how we might best prepare to avoid becoming the victim of crime. Fear is an innate instinct that is intended to protect us from harm. Unwarranted fear, however, restricts our freedom to live daily lives as we choose.

Some people perceive danger where there is none. Others ignore danger signs when they should be obvious. Somewhere in between these extremes a balance needs to be discovered. Although many women fear becoming the victim of a rape or attempted rape, these crimes are "...relatively rare crimes compared to robbery and assault, accounting for less than 3% of all violent crime measured...."[11]

Perception of Danger

Our ability to perceive danger is based upon many factors: Self-awareness, environmental awareness, past experiences, observation abilities or limitations, frame of reference, pre-existing fears, and problem-solving abilities. "If you are unable to identify your own feelings or gauge other people's intentions, you may not recognize danger. If you space out, you may be oblivious to warning signals. And if you freeze when you're frightened, it will be harder

---

[11]"Female Victims of Violent Crime," U.S. Department of Justice, Office of Justice Programs, Bureau of Justice Statistics, by Caroline Wolf Harlow, Ph.D., January 1991, NCJ-12826, p. 7.

to act appropriately."[12]

Ann's experience illustrates this point. Her parents were vacationing in Florida and made arrangements for Ann to periodically check their home. It was late afternoon when Ann pulled into the driveway and clicked her remote-control electric garage door opener. As the door opened, Ann saw that the door into the house was standing open.

Ann was startled. This door was closed the last time she saw it. Ann inquisitively inspected the interior of the house and soon realized that the home had been burglarized. Only then did she summon the police. Not until later did Ann realize the potentially dangerous situation she placed herself in by entering the house alone. She had recognized the obvious warning signs of a burglary, but neglected her own safety. Ann's initial concern about her parent's property clouded her ability to recognize potential danger to herself.

The ability to perceive danger can be improved with experience. Police officers become quite adept at recognizing danger signals in the people and situations they encounter. Appraisal of what constitutes danger involves recognizing that all of the senses play a significant role. If you "have a feeling" that something is not right, it probably isn't. That "feeling" is your sixth sense, which you may not be fully conscious of, signalling your body to take action. Common danger signals:

1. **Body signals:** Perspiration, increased heart rate, and an adrenaline rush are all physiological reactions to fear. Recognize these body reactions and determine what has triggered these responses. Trust your instincts!

---

[12]Ellen Bass and Laura Davis, *The Courage to Heal, A Guide for Women Survivors of Child Sexual Abuse* (Harper and Rowe, 1988), p. 221.

2. **Out of place:** Look for what is out of place in the environment, not what is normal and expected. The old saying, "What is wrong with this picture?" is a good rule for evaluating what is out of place. The van in your neighbor's driveway while they are away may belong there, but possibly does not. The two young men loitering near the entrance of the shopping center may not intend to steal a purse. Then again, they might. The very young man driving an expensive car through your neighborhood may not be a young thief in a stolen car, but quite possibly he is. When similar conditions occur to you, initiate your own powers of investigation. This is not intended to have you play police officer, only to be more inquisitive in a safe way. Take note and take notes, call the police, ask another person about the circumstances you have observed, or inquire in some other manner. Chances are, this inquisitive nature will pay off.

3. **Be suspicious:** A little dose of healthy suspicion should not hurt, and may help. Don't assume that people who call and call upon you are who they say they are. Confirm information through questions and documentation of the caller's claims. Being suspicious means a heightened state of awareness as you interact with others. As you become skilled at "reading" other people you will find valuable information is delivered from their nonverbal messages. If there are any incongruities, the nonverbal messages tend to belie the spoken word.

4. **Look Up!** You will miss danger signals from your environment unless you physically and mentally "look up." Defensive driving is to survival on the roadways as "defensive" walking is to survival in our communities. Cautious drivers are concerned with

much more than where the car is being steered. They are constantly looking to the side, rear and far down the road for danger signals. Similar methods while walking, shopping, and otherwise traveling will pay dividends in recognition of danger.

5.   *Panic Reactions:* A panic reaction to danger signals may not be an appropriate course of action. To *panic* means to be out of control and without a plan. Earlier suggestions of playing "what if" scenarios can serve to elicit a more patterned response to danger signals. The reason for fire drills in schools is to minimize the panic response of school children in the event of an actual fire.

Summary

Perception *is* reality when it comes to behavioral responses. If your perception is accurate, your responses will be appropriate. If your perception is inaccurate, inappropriate actions are likely to result. Perceptions result when our observations of the environment are "filtered" through our frame of reference. Fear is a natural reaction to stress and danger and is intended to protect us. The perception of danger is a product of fear and our frame of reference. The ability to perceive danger accurately is a skill and can be enhanced through accurate observations and reflection upon those observations.

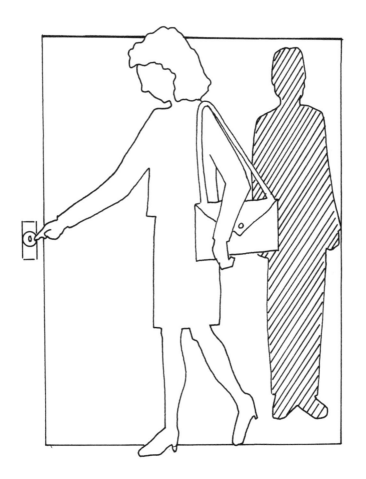

3. The Rape Attack: Resist Or Submit

"Different motives operate in different offenders.... (Tactics) successful in dissuading one type of assailant might...

aggravate the situation with a
different type offender."[1]

Personal Risk Analysis

Should you fight back or submit in the rape
situation? There is no best solution or a single technique
that can be guaranteed to always work. The research of
Federal Bureau of Investigation (FBI) Agents Robert
Hazelwood and Joseph H. Harpold indicate:

> There is no one specific way to deal with a rape
> situation.... We offer confrontational advice only if
> we have specific information about three critical
> variables: 1) the environment of the assault; 2) an
> understanding of certain personality characteristics
> of the victim; and 3) the type of motivation of the
> rapist involved.[2]

The rape confrontation requires good decision-
making ability, not emotional based rhetoric, as the source
for reaction. We teach three critical variables as the
fundamental first steps in *Personal Risk Analysis:*

1. Consider the Environment of the Attack

The location and hour of the day when the attack
occurs will influence how you respond. "The advice one
would provide to a victim encountering a rapist in a
shopping mall parking lot at 4:00 p.m. would certainly differ
from the advice given for an encounter occurring on a
deserted roadway."[3] A tactic such as screaming may be

---

[1]*Providing Confrontation Advise,* FBI Law Enforcement
Bulletin, Vol. 55, No. 6, June 1986, pp. 1-5.

[2]Ibid.

[3]Ibid.

successful in the first encounter, but not in the latter.

Consider the following environmental descriptions for personal risk analysis:

a.   Working alone in the workplace after business hours.
b.   Experiencing a vehicle breakdown in an isolated or unfamiliar area.
c.   Walking alone to your vehicle in the parking lot at night.
d.   Jogging alone.

Personal Risk Analysis seeks to identify environmental factors that increase the likelihood that you will become a crime victim, and then to evaluate tactics for successful counter-measures.

2.   *Understand Your Own Personality*

It is hard for a passive person to be assertive or physically aggressive in self-defense. It is equally difficult for a person with an aggressive personality to be passive in self-defense. It is essential that you carefully examine your personal behavior patterns (passive, assertive, aggressive) and then honestly ask:

a.   *What would I like to do in a rape situation?*   This question asks you to seriously examine the type of responses you would apply in a rape encounter. Will you use a weapon, physical, non-physical alternatives, or some combination of these responses? No one else can choose the correct response(s) for you. These are individual choices that only you can make to ensure success in the event of an attack.

b.   *What could I realistically do in a rape situation?* This question is designed to force you to seriously consider personal risk analysis as a path to understanding your psychological strengths and weaknesses in rape attack situations.

i.   **Psychological:** People are not all alike. One woman in a rape encounter may feel she has survived because she is "going home alive" after the attack. Another woman may never shake the emotional distress of the experience.

    Many factors influence our values, principles, and belief systems. Support groups will vary, and recovery from being a crime victim is uniquely individual. In addition, the consideration to use force when under attack is certain for some women, and absolutely unacceptable for others. It is interesting that mothers may hesitate to use physical force when assaulted by a male, yet they do not hesitate to use physical force to protect a child.

ii.   **Physical:** Women, as well as men, need to conduct a personal risk analysis to determine a realistic understanding of what they could actually do in a physical confrontation. Responses include fighting, struggling, and wrestling techniques.

    Males tend to practice what we refer to as locker-room boasting. This *verbalization* is merely emotionally attacking windmills without realistically considering individual physical capabilities and limitations in actually performing the task.

    Visualization is a better method. Instead of mere locker-room boasting, visualization means to mentally practice realistic "what if" scenarios. In your visualizing, methodically track potential courses of action for a confrontation situation. For example, in general you can assume that the rapist will be physically stronger than you. If you believe this, it will influence your consideration and what will likely be the most effective self-defense alternatives.

3. Consider the Motivation of the Rapist

We agree with Agents Hazelwood and Harpold that this variable is the "most important unknown." Recall the earlier statement, "different motives operate in different offenders." Recognize that a specific tactic may frighten one attacker, yet motivate another, to the escalation of violence in the attack.

Deviant Behavior author Erich Goode cites research (Groth, 1979) which studied the motives and psychological characteristic of rapists. The research found three distinct types of rapes: anger rapes, power rapes, and sadistic rapes.[4]

The *anger* rapist attacks his victim, grabs her, strikes her, knocks her to the ground and beats her as a way to express rage. The desire of the *power* rapist is to harm his victim physically, to master, to control, to show authority, and so on. The *sadistic* rapist intends to torture his victim. Punishment and destruction is part of his method of operation.[5]

"Any or all of the suggested tactic for either passive or active, can work under the right set of circumstances,

---

[4]E. Goode, *Deviant Behavior* (Englewood Cliffs, New Jersey: Prentice-Hall, Inc., 1984), p. 240.

[5]Ibid.

but none are guaranteed to be effective in all situations."[6]

There is no one best answer to questions about what to do or how to behave in an assaultive situation. The best advice is to be prepared by learning a wide variety of alternatives backed by sound decision-making so that proper actions can be taken when needed. Every situation is difficult and controlled by many factors which cannot be analyzed before-the-fact in a simplistic fashion.

What if the Rapist Has a Weapon?

As you already know, advice regarding the "one best" course of action doesn't exist. The unfair burden to interpret the rapist's motivation and select an appropriate course of action is placed on the shoulders of the victim.

Your major concern in this situation is to prevent what is intended to be a rape from escalating to greater injury or death. The two true stories below clarify this point:

Sue

Sue (not her real name) had just finished buying the weekly groceries. It was after dark. Sue was carrying the bags of food into the house from her car. Her car was parked in the driveway. An assailant approached, wielding a handgun. He ordered Sue into her home where she was raped. The assailant left after the rape. Sue choose not to resist the attack and did "survive" in that she was not seriously injured considering the potential for injury.

Joe

Joe (not his real name) was a store clerk working the midnight shift at a convenience store. He was alone in the store. A lone gunman entered and ordered Joe to hand

---

[6]J. Delipsey, S.K. James and M. D. Fleming, "Rape Defense: A Complex Issue," Prevention Press, Winter 1982, pp. 4-5.

over the money. Joe reached down. He picked up a baseball bat which he kept behind the counter for "self-protection." As Joe raised the bat over his head to strike the robber, the robber shot and killed Joe.

Decisions made by the victim can have consequences which were possibly not intended by the criminal. Increase your chances of survival by giving careful thought to the three critical variables discussed in this chapter. Select alternatives that are appropriate for you, and practice the techniques until they come naturally or from second nature. Even then, we offer no guarantees. Your attacker will most likely know more about fighting and the use of intimidation than you do.

Law enforcement officers are trained to develop skills to interpret non-verbal and verbal behavior when confronting suspects. With years of experience they develop the ability to note cues that alert them to danger. However, even with all of the training and experience, there is no guarantee that police officers will successfully survive an encounter where the suspect has a weapon.

If You Should Become a Rape Victim
The following recommendations are offered as a way to help law enforcement officers identify, arrest and seek prosecution of the rapist:

1.   Immediately contact the local law enforcement agency. The vast majority of law enforcement officers are trained to be understanding to your situation and will have support referral agencies for you to contact.

2.   As difficult as it must sound, write down facts about the incident. Describe the rapist and other circumstances of the assault.

3. Do not bathe, wash your hands, douche, change clothes, or tend to other matters of personal hygiene. This preserves any evidence that may exist on your person. This is extremely difficult to tolerate for most rape victims, but it greatly improves the chances of arrest and successful prosecution.

4. The law enforcement officer will need to interview you. Law enforcement agencies have become extremely sensitive to the crime of rape and the emotional well-being of the victim. Although the rape circumstances may be embarrassing and unpleasant to talk about, they are a necessary part of the police investigation.

5. You will be asked by the law enforcement officer to seek medical attention immediately at the hospital. A physician's examination is necessary for your physical well-being, and it will help in the police investigation.

6. Ask about area agencies who will assist in counseling.

7. If you should remember important information about the incident days or weeks after the attack, report it to the investigating agency.

We wish to summarize the points of this chapter with two stories which illustrate that the decision to resist or submit to the demands of a rapist cannot be made by anyone but the victim. You alone must assess the situation and choose how you will respond.

Mary
Mary is a 55-year-old woman who describes herself as the "grandmother" type. She is single and is always

concerned with the potential of becoming a crime victim. As a shift supervisor for nearly 20 years at a plastics factory, she is accustomed to administering discipline to both men and women, and has developed an aggressive style of life.

One evening as Mary returned to her car in the parking lot of a large department store, a young, suspicious-looking man approached her. As Mary reached her car, the man came "too" close. Mary glared at the man, boldly presented her right fist (that held her protruding car keys) and stated, "What do you want?!" The young man stopped, looked toward the ground, then began walking away. He suddenly stopped and again walked toward Mary.

Mary was sure that this man intended to take her purse, or possibly attempt to rape her. She felt that he was undecided how, or if, he was to commit the crime. As the man approached Mary again she raised her voice, shook her fist at him and yelled, "Stop! I am prepared to defend myself!" The man turned and ran into the shadows. On the way home, Mary stopped at the police station and gave a full account.

Mary made a decision and employed a strategy based on her own mental and physical confidence. This appears to have been the best course of action for Mary, for it was both natural and convincing.

Sarah

Sarah was 75 years of age when she was physically assaulted and raped in her home. "Stop! I have AIDS!" Sarah told the man.

The rapist, a man in his early 20's, replied, "That's okay, so do I," and he proceeded with his crime.

Sarah's strategy failed, Mary's was a success. But in different circumstances Sarah's strategy may have worked and Mary's failed. There are no guarantees. It is wise to read about different strategies that have worked, but naive to think your chances for success are great unless you practice the strategies you choose to use.

There are many factors influencing the outcome of an attack. The great unknown factor is how you will react, and what defense strategies will be at your disposal, in a rape situation.

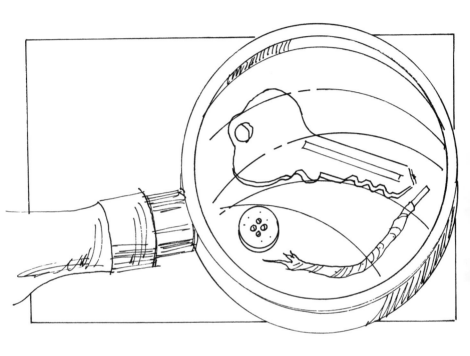

4. *Observation And Awareness*

Most people are not trained
observers. They observe many
people they encounter without
actually perceiving their

physical characteristics and
other traits.[1]

Observation is a skill that may not come naturally, but can be learned and practiced. This chapter introduces you to the value of improving personal powers of observation and offers techniques to enhance this skill. These techniques provide a framework of information, practice exercises, and self-instruction strategies.

The Need
Most people are preoccupied with a host of thoughts, demands, and concerns while walking, shopping, driving, and communicating on a day-to-day basis. We have a tendency toward *looking at*, instead of *seeing* the people, places and events before us.

Good observation skills provide us with more accurate information to make better preventive decisions. To illustrate this point, consider a story provided by one of our students while travelling in Africa:

A young female was walking alone down a poorly lighted alley. Excited about being a student in Africa and her studies, she was preoccupied with the challenges and activities scheduled for the following day. Suddenly she became aware of two men approaching her.

This young lady recalled the authors' remarks about observation and awareness. She immediately shifted her posture to an erect (assertive) state, and increased her gait. She concentrated her eyes on the movement of the approaching men. She fought negative thoughts of **Why am I walking alone?** *to focus on where she was in relation to doorways, escape routes, or other people passing on the sidewalk hundreds of feet ahead.*

---

[1]Thomas F. Adams, *Police Patrol Tactics and Techniques* (Englewood, N.J., Prentice-Hall Inc., 1971), pp. 84-89.

The two men lunged at her. One man choked her from behind. She struggled until a knife was pressed to her throat. She then chose to adapt by relaxing and allowing the backpack she was carrying to fall off her shoulder. Immediately the backpack was grabbed away and she was pushed to the ground. She walked away shaken, but virtually unharmed. She survived the encounter. It should also be noted that her money and important papers were in a wallet carried in a pants pocket.

This incident illustrates three importance facts:

1.   Observation skills play a key role in detecting suspicious or potentially dangerous situations.
2.   Awareness training can assist in gaining a sense of self-control.
3.   Shifting from a preoccupied state of mind leads to a more alert defensive mental posture.

What Is Observation?

A dictionary definition of observation might read, "an act or power of observing; the gathering of information by noting facts or circumstances."

The authors define observation as the act of being alert, attentive and aware of people and activities in your environment. It requires that you not merely *look,* but also *see.* Here is a story that illustrates the difference between looking and seeing:

The Recruit Police Officer

While on patrol, a recruit officer was instructed by her Field Training Officer (FTO) to inspect the security of a closed business. She used a spotlight to ensure that the store had not been burglarized. It was dark, and the recruit officer shined the spotlight on the large window which gave an immediate reflection. The recruit officer confidently responded, "The building has not been broken into."

47

The FTO waited a moment, then began to quiz the recruit officer about her observations. "Is the floor-safe door open or closed?"

The recruit officer smiled, thought the FTO was joking, and half-heartedly responded, "What floor-safe?"

The FTO repositioned the patrol vehicle in front of the store window, focused the spotlight on the window, and informatively instructed, "Don't merely LOOK at the window, SEE through it."

The recruit officer first noticed the reflection of the spotlight, then concentrated her vision by seeing through the window and observing the vault floor-safe door standing wide open. The floor-safe had been burglarized several years prior and the owner never bothered to have it repaired.

The floor-safe was commonly used as a training aid by FTOs wanting to make a strong point about observation to trainees. The recruit officer fell victim to common foes of accurate observation: becoming preoccupied and rushing her observation process.

This recruit officer learned a valuable lesson that evening. The act of looking takes place routinely, and provides a limited picture to the viewer.

How We Observe: The Act of Seeing

We know the importance of our five senses in making observations, decisions and conclusions about the world we live in. The five senses are seeing, hearing, smelling, touching, and tasting. Becoming an accurate observer requires more than seeing with just our eyes. The following story demonstrates the art of seeing:

A Handicap/A Strength

A young boy sat on the grass in the park with his elderly grandfather. The grandfather had been blind since he was ten years old. After resting a few minutes the grandfather said to his grandson, "This is such a beautiful

48

day. Look -- the sun is bright, but the sky is cloudy. Listen to the pigeons on the concession-stand roof. See the geese swimming in the water. How beautiful are the lilies. How happily the lady is pushing the children in the swing. The grass is long and requires cutting soon."

The young boy hastily interrupted his grandfather and said, "Grandfather, I do not understand, for you have seen things I did not notice until you mentioned them. I can see with my eyes, but you can not."

It is helpful to pause for a moment and ask a few questions about our story:

1. How did the blind grandfather accurately observe his surroundings? What senses did he use?
2. Do you think most people routinely observe like the grandfather, or more like the grandson?

Seeing accurately requires a conscious effort to use all five senses, but accuracy can be hampered by barriers. The following quotation provides insight into barriers affecting accurate observations:

The observations and descriptions of witnesses may not be detailed nor objective as those made by trained observers like investigators. Trained observers know that their observations can be affected by lack of sleep, illness, or by other outside influences.... Environmental factors like weather and light can influence what people see.... Emotions like fear, anger, or worry and mental set like prejudice or irrational thinking patterns may impair perceptions.[2]

Preoccupation can serve as a visual and perception

---

[2]*Law Enforcement Investigator*, Headquarter, Department of Army FM 19-20, Washington, D.C., 1985, pp. 33-34.

blinder. It limits what we see and consequently how we react. Physical impairments of vision and hearing can also limit and impact the accuracy of the information received. These are but a few of the barriers that can influence accurate observation of people, objects and events. The following story demonstrates factors positively and negatively influencing observation:

The Larceny

Evening slowly encompassed the shopping mall as a scattering of shoppers hurried to and from their cars on this cool summer evening. The front of the mall was well lighted. However, the parking lot illumination was just beginning to reach full power.

Chained to one of the mall support pillars was a man's blue 10-speed bicycle. A young man approached the bicycle as the foyer temporally cleared of shoppers. This person was 16 years old, wearing a white sailor's cap, blue denim jacket and jeans, and was wearing red jogging shoes. His brown hair reached to his shoulders and when the wind blew just right, the earring in his left ear was exposed. His name is Jim.

A second young man also approached the bicycle. The second young man was also 16 years old and was wearing a University shirt, yellow shorts and brown sandals. This young man was named Freddie and had a flat top hair cut.

Jim bent over the bicycle and used wire cutters to cut the thin chain which secured the bicycle. As Jim cut the chain, Freddie exclaimed, "Jim, don't do it." Jim freed the bicycle, got on it and rode away with Freddie running after him.

Three people witnessed the larceny of the bicycle. A police officer was summoned after the owner discovered his bicycle had been stolen.

Witness one, Glenn, is a 45-year-old retired United

States Navy man who is currently employed as a city recreation counselor. Glenn served twenty-two years as a sports and recreation coordinator for the Navy. Glenn is nearsighted and was not wearing glasses at the time the bicycle was stolen. Glenn was approximately thirty feet from the bicycle when it was stolen.

The second witness, Helen, a 33-year-old mother of two boys, is employed full-time as a truant officer in the local high school. Helen's father is a police officer. Helen suffers from a slight hearing loss and was not wearing her prescribed hearing aid at the time of the incident. Helen was standing about forty feet from the bicycle when it was stolen.

The third witness, Clara, a 16-year-old, has two teenaged brothers. Clara is interested in being a fashion designer after college and is currently employed in one of the women's stores in the mall. Clara was standing only a few feet from the bicycle at the time it was stolen.

The police officer interviewed Glenn first. Glenn gave the following account: *I saw two boys standing near the English racing bike. Both boys looked very young to me, perhaps they were fourteen or fifteen years old. I can't remember what kind of jackets or pants they were wearing, but one boy was wearing a sailor's cap, an enlisted man's cap. As the first boy (with the sailor's cap) got onto the bike and road away, the other boy stated "Jim, or Tim, don't do this." That second boy sure could run. I would like to have him on my track team.*

Helen saw things a little bit differently. She told the police officer: *All I can recall is one boy, who looks familiar by the way, was shady looking. I'm sure that he has been in trouble with the law before. The boy who actually stole the bike had long dirty hair that needs to be washed. All that I heard them say was "Jim don't use that gun." I'm sure that they are both old enough to be in the 10th grade, unless they have flunked a few grades.*

Clara told the police officer: *The two boys who*

stole the bicycle are the age of my oldest brother and he is
16. The boy who rode away on the bicycle was wearing
Bugle Boy jeans and jacket and had on Nike red tennis
shoes. I'm sure the second boy gets his hair cut in the mall
at Harper's Barber Shop, because his is the only shop in
town doing that style now. The second boy was wearing
brown sandals, which look tacky, by the way.

All three witnesses observed the same event,
although from different physical and mental vantage points.
Which witness had the most accurate description of the
events and persons involved? What barriers may have been
underlying the various accounts that were given to the
police officer? What additional questions would you ask of
the witnesses if you were the police officer assigned to
perform this investigation and write the police report?

FACTS: Tips for Developing Observation Skills
These techniques are offered to help you enhance
your ability to focus, to become more attentive, and recall
your observation when needed. The acronym FACTS refers
to Face, Age, Clothing, Talk, and Shape. With practice you
can train yourself to quickly recall the FACTS.

*F*ace: Focus on the forehead, eyebrows, facial hair,
ears, cheeks, nose, mouth, lips, teeth, chin, jaw, scars,
glasses, hat, etc. Think of people you know for comparison
purposes.

*A*ge: Guessing at an approximate age, whether
young or old, may be too global and depends upon your
frame of reference. Think in terms of people who you
know for comparison purposes.

*C*lothing: Look at the hat, jacket, pants, shoes,
gloves, and shirt. Note the cleanliness of clothing, how it is

worn, and distinguishing characteristics. These details are helpful in later identification of a particular person.

Talk: Note the language, accent, vocabulary, profanity, threats, specific statements, nervousness, humor, and other vocal traits.

Shape: Is the face and body shape oval, round, or rectangular? Note the type of build: tall, short, stocky, average weight, whatever.

By thinking of the FACTS you will be able to focus your attention on observation and be able to recall later what you have observed.

Objects

Objects require the description of items such as vehicles, guns, knives, office equipment, and so on. The difficulty associated with making an accurate observation of objects is primarily one of unfamiliarity. For example, if a person is not a hunter or marksman, he or she may not know the difference between a rifle, shotgun, and revolver. A key to improving observation skill is the willingness to broaden your personal interest knowledge bank.

Vehicles can best be observed and recalled through the use of the acronym CYMBAL:

(C)olor
(Y)ear
(M)ake
(B)ody
(A)nd
(L)icense

This same method is taught in police academies to law enforcement officers to systematically obtain descriptions and focus attention toward better observation and recall of automobiles.

Over time, each automobile becomes distinctive to others of similar make and model, so it is also important to note any dents, missing parts, decals, personalized license plates or other unique features.

Events

Events are best remembered in chronological order of their occurrence. Suspicious acts often leave the observer uncertain of exactly what happened. Most often, the feeling that "something is not right" or "what is wrong with this picture" occurs to the observer.

A suspicious event could be a vehicle parked in your neighbor's driveway with the motor running and you realize that the motor does not sound like your neighbor's. Other suspicious activities could be the sound of glass breaking or of a person screaming or yelling.

Many persons hesitate to take note of suspicious events, or to notify the police or other neighbors. It is helpful if you immediately jot notes about the events that you witnessed. Remember to use FACTS and CYMBAL in your report. Also try to answer the questions every newspaper reporter is trained to ask: WHO, WHAT, WHEN, WHERE, WHY, and HOW.

Preventive Decision Making

Our society is a busy one. People move about their home, workplace, travel, and recreation in a frequent state of preoccupation. While driving home, thoughts might be on the evening meal, tomorrow's work duties, or the band concert that starts in an hour. In short, much of our thought process is dealing with the *future*.

Preoccupation can interfere with safety and preventive decision-making as it can distract attention and result in a bad decision or accident. For example, a defensive driver recognizes that being alert with full concentration upon the actions of other drivers and the driving environment is the key to accident avoidance.

Accident prevention is the goal of defensive driving, with mental concentration upon the tasks at hand as the key to defensive driving. Observation skills can be the key to fostering a Personal Defense Posture designed to "reduce the opportunity of becoming a victim of crime."

Observation skills require awareness of our surroundings wherever we might be and to be alert to suspicious people, objects and events. Evasive action can only follow personal recognition of a threatening situation.

Observation Skill Exercises

The following games will help you hone observation skills. The key to improving any skill is practice, practice and practice. It is also helpful if the practice is fun and easy to do.

The Road Game

This game improves observation skills while driving or riding in a car. This exercise can be done on either long or short trips, while in the car alone or with others. Caution must be taken not to lose concentration on the task of driving while playing this game.

Start by looking for a unique feature about the car in front of you. This feature should be one that distinguishes that vehicle from another of similar make, color and style -- a dent, bumper sticker, decal, etc.

If others are participating in the game, a leader is designated and makes note of a particular feature of the "target" vehicle. The others must observe and guess which feature has been chosen by the leader. Honesty and fair play are important.

Other Road Games

CAUTION: Do not concentrate on these games to the extent that you ignore your responsibility to drive defensively.

License Plate -- This game involves remembering the license number of a vehicle that passes yours, or that you pass. The leader will describe the "target" vehicle and the others must recall the license plate number and the state that the plate is from. Since time-lapse and other communication can hamper the ability to recall, allow some time to pass before challenging the other player to recall the license number.

Exit Vehicle -- Ask others, or challenge yourself, to describe the car that exited the freeway at the last exit ramp.

Pedestrian -- After passing a hitchhiker or pedestrian, attempt to give a complete description of that person (using FACTS).

The Shopping Game

The shopping game can also be played alone or with others. *Caution:* Do not lose concentration and forget what it was that you went to the store to purchase!

Describe, or ask someone with you to describe, the mannequin in the store window that you just passed.

After leaving the store, describe the person who was waiting ahead of you in the checkout lane. Describe the person who was waiting behind you in the checkout lane. Describe the cashier who waited on you.

The Radio Game

After a sportscast, try to recall as many of the teams who played and the scores of the games as possible. What was the name of the sportscaster? What products were advertised during the commercials?

Listen to, and recall as much of the weather forecast as possible, including the barometric pressure, temperature in other areas, and so on.

To test your skill, tape record the broadcast and replay it to review your success.

The Television Game

Describe the clothing worn by an actor on a television program. Concentrate on actors who do not play lead roles and only appear in "walk-on" or minor roles.

Try to recall and repeat something an actor said during a particular segment of the show.

A video recording of the show will demonstrate your skill level and observation accuracy.

The Work/School Game

Write down a complete description of a person who has just walked out of the office, classroom, or work area. Check the accuracy of your description when you next see that person.

When walking into work or school, try to remember the description of a co-worker or schoolmate's vehicle, including the license number. See if you can retain this knowledge throughout the day's activities.

The Mall Game

The next time you shop at the mall, sit on a bench and observe people shopping and walking. This exercise can be valuable in two ways:

First, it provides an opportunity to practice the FACTS acronym. Focus on an individual for 15 to 30 seconds, then look down. Looking down helps you maintain focus and concentrate solely on your observation. As you look down, recall your observation by mentally working through the FACTS:

Face
Age
Clothes
Talk
Shape

The more you practice using this acronym in conjunction with observations, the easier it becomes to focus, concentrate, and recall your observation.

Secondly, this exercise is a real-life study of human behavior. Observe people for the purpose of noting nonverbal cues that communicate such things as feelings, energy levels, assertiveness, and attitudes. Ask yourself the following questions:

? Is the person, while standing or walking, communicating a submissive, assertive, or aggressive behavior?

? What observations lead you to believe that certain behaviors or attitudes are being communicated?

? Are others observant of you and your behaviors?

? Are others guilty of poor crime prevention habits during their shopping? Is their purse unattended, are they flashing money, etc.

The Picture Game

This exercise can be practiced anywhere that a picture or photograph is available for viewing. Focus on a picture hanging on a wall or in a magazine or book for 15 to 30 seconds. Be attentive to detail (people, location, objects and activities). Immediately look down to retain concentration and recall what you observed.

Author's Surprise Test [No Cheating!]

1. How many people are depicted on the cover drawing of this book? Describe the person(s). How many people do you perceive as potential victims or attackers?

2. Describe the setting or location depicted in the drawing.

3. What activity, if any, is depicted in the drawing that would cause a preventive oriented person to become suspicious?

4. What preventive strategies would you recommend for the potential victim(s) in the drawing?

5. Now (if you haven't already done so) turn to the drawing and compare your observation recall with the picture. How did you do?

These are but a few examples of games that can help you improve observation skills. It is easy to make up your own game and involve the family, co-workers, or schoolmates. The key to improvement of observation skills is desire and practice.

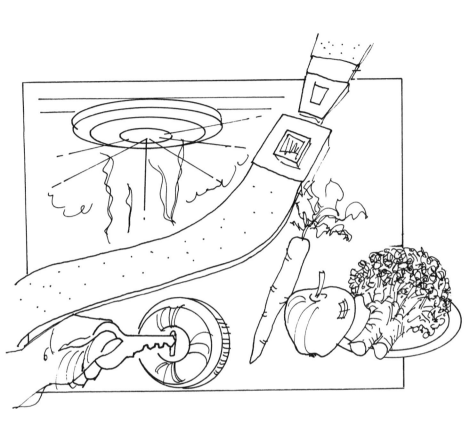

5. Preventive Strategies

Educating and alerting people
how they can reduce their
vulnerability to the crimes about
them is a continuing
responsibility of law

enforcement, and it is as
necessary as a patrol force.[1]

Strategies

There are specific techniques and strategies that
have the potential to minimize the chances of becoming
victimized. While there are no guarantees that these
techniques will always work, specialists in communities
throughout the United States have reported crime reduction
in neighborhoods where active prevention programs are in
operation.

The following recommendations introduce some
crime prevention strategies for you to integrate into your
daily lifestyle. For a more complete list, check with your
local police department for free printed crime prevention
pamphlets and literature.

1. Your Home

Conduct a risk analysis survey of your home. A first
step would be to inquire with your local police department
about receiving a free premises survey to identify strengths
and weaknesses regarding the doors, locks, lighting,
windows, alarms, and so on. (This service may not be
available in all communities.)

Seriously consider becoming involved in a
neighborhood watch program. If your neighborhood isn't
currently participating in the program, consider becoming a
Neighborhood Watch Group Leader, and implement a
program in your neighborhood.

"Lock" sliding glass doors by placing a wood or
metal rod in the track behind the door to prevent it from
opening. Be careful not to create a fire trap by firmly

---

[1]Federal Bureau of Investigation, *Crime Resistance*
(Washington, D.C.: U.S. Government Printing Office, 1977),
p. 5.

wedging the wood into the track. The wood need only to fit loosely, so that it can be removed from the inside quickly and easily. Be sure to educate your children how to exit the house in a hurry in case of an emergency.

Trim shrubs and trees around doors and windows to eliminate hiding places for burglars and prowlers. Put yourself into the frame of mind of a crook looking for a place of concealment near your home and let this be your guide to what vegetation might need to be trimmed or removed.

Never leave messages which can inform a burglar that your home is unoccupied, such as allowing newspapers and mail to pile up. Instead, hold delivery on these items, or have a friend retrieve them daily. Never tape messages to the door announcing you are not home, such as, "Bob -- gone to the store, will be back at 6:00 p.m."

Resist leaving the house key in obvious places, such as under the door mat, in the mailbox, or above the door. Be more creative if a hiding place for your key is necessary.

Consider installing an automatic garage door opener to reduce the exposure to outside threats as you enter or leave your garage, particularly at night. Make sure that garage door controls are out of the reach of children, so that an injury is not caused by playing with the controls.

Always try to foster the impression that someone is home. Leave selected lights on, use a timer for lights, play the radio or television, and so on. One burglar admitted that whenever he encountered a bathroom door partially closed, with the fan and light in operation, he was fairly certain someone was home and would immediately leave.

Always be cautious of allowing strangers into your home. A request to use a telephone to call a wrecker service or some other emergency may be legitimate, or it may be a ploy to victimize you. Keep the door closed and offer to make the call for them. Do not hesitate to ask for the identification of a person representing themselves as from the power company, cable television company, or police department. Our experience is that people are generally too trusting of strangers who knock at their door.

A 1991 U.S. Department of Justice study entitled Female Victims of Violent Crimes, reported: "Most rapes occurred at home. Four in ten completed rapes took place at the victim's home. Two in ten occurred near a friend's home, and two in ten on the street."[2]

This study examined reported rapes for a fifteen-year period: "From 1973 to 1987, there were annually 1.6 rapes per 1,000 women age twelve or older, meaning that one out of every 600 women was a rape victim each year."[3]

This information is offered not to frighten you, but to motivate you to take the steps listed above to prevent such a crime from happening to you, in or near your home.

2. Your Car

Traveling in your car can increase your exposure to becoming a crime victim. Try to keep your vehicle in good running condition and keep plenty of gasoline in the gas tank.

Always keep your vehicle doors locked to prevent an unwanted person from entering while stopped at a traffic signal. Another reason to keep your doors locked is to minimize the chances of the door flying open during an accident.

If your vehicle breaks down, remain inside, lock all doors, put on the flashers, and roll up all of the windows. Realize that the flashers might attract either a helpful

---

[2]"Female Victims of Crime," U.S. Department of Justice, Office of Justice Programs, Bureau of Justice Statistics, by Caroline Wolf Harlow, Ph.D, BJS Statistician, January, 1991, NCJ126826, p. 7.

[3]Ibid.

person, or a potential rapist. Keep windows up and ask the person to call the police for you. At a time like this, preplanning may put communication with others at your fingertips in the form of a CB radio or cellular phone.

Keep adequate change available in your vehicle for telephone calls. Remember, 911 calls do not normally require money at pay phones. Keep a list of emergency phone numbers in your purse or glove compartment.

Never pick up hitchhikers. A mugger, robber, or rapist could look like the boy next door. Render assistance to other stranded motorists by stopping at the nearest phone to report the vehicle breakdown.

Keep valuable items in the trunk or out of sight while shopping. The packages are best left in the trunk.

Before entering a parked vehicle, always look for a person hiding underneath the vehicle, inside the vehicle, or standing suspiciously nearby. Some of our students report that they never park next to a van or other view-blocking vehicle for fear of being assaulted when entering or exiting their car.

Strongly consider installing a CB or cellular phone for emergency purposes.

3. Walking

Walking and jogging are popular forms of recreation and fitness for people of all ages. Unfortunately, such activities also increase your chances of becoming a crime victim. When walking or jogging, take the precautions outlined below.

Plan your route and know what stores are open if you should require emergency assistance. Choose the most populated route.

When possible, and especially at night, do not walk alone. Walking or jogging with another person could deter a crime.

Maintain a confident, alert walking pace and posture. This will most likely send a signal to a potential attacker that you are alert and assertive. One of our students, when she perceived a potential threat, would look ahead of her, wave and acknowledge a non-existent person while speeding up her gate.

Being alert (see the chapter on observation skills) includes being aware of the people, vehicles, and activities surrounding you. If you note someone staring at you, look that person in the eye briefly to acknowledge that you are also aware of his or her presence.

In an area where vehicles are parked, keep note of the vehicles that are unlocked. If you believe you are being followed, enter the unlocked vehicle and lock the doors, then honk the horn to attract the attention of others.

Be cautious of people seeking directions and always keep a safe distance from their vehicle.

4. Shopping

Shopping is an environment which can make women vulnerable to crime. Even though both men and women shop, a much higher ratio of women are in the typical store at any given time.

Wearing expensive clothing, furs, and jewelry may signal to the would-be criminal that you are affluent and a worthwhile target for a crime.

Remain alert to the people near you. Hold your purse firmly and close to your body. Note: Wrapping the purse strap around your wrist to prevent its loss can be dangerous and possibly result in being pulled to the ground and injured. We recommend that you carry your wallet (including cash, credit cards and keys) in an alternate place such as a coat pocket. This way, if you must let go of the purse to a mugger, you will keep possession of your valuables.

Keep a minimum of cash on you and only the credit cards you need for shopping. Never display large sums of cash in public view. If your credit cards or checkbook are lost or stolen, report them immediately to the police agency of jurisdiction and then to the appropriate financial institutions.

Never leave your purse unattended on a counter, or leave packages unattended in dressing rooms or the rest room.

Shopping often creates a hurried state of mind and in such a state we are prone to forgetting about our surroundings and potential threats. We recommend that you *slow down*, and *remain alert.*

Remember, the shopping period between the holidays of Thanksgiving and Christmas are a prime time for the crime of purse snatching. Purse snatchers realize that most shoppers will be carrying more cash than normal this time of year. The muggers might be surprised by your advanced preparation.

5. Parking Lot

The parking lot should be considered a vulnerable environment during both day and evening hours.

When possible, park in spaces close to the stores you will shop and near lighted areas during the evening hours.

When leaving the store, walk directly to your vehicle with your car keys in your hand. Push your packages in a cart when available. The cart can become a weapon and aid in keeping a would-be attacker distanced. The cart also keeps your hands free of packages, as the sight of a woman heavily loaded with packages in the parking lot could make a likely target.

When returning to your vehicle, immediately observe the vicinity of your vehicle for any suspicious activity such as people gathering near your vehicle. Check underneath and look inside your vehicle before opening the door. Immediately put your packages in the vehicle, enter while being observant, and lock the doors.

While leaving the shopping area, or whenever driving, frequently check your rear-view mirror to ensure that no one is following you. We are not trying to make you paranoid. However, it is a good practice to regularly be observant of your surroundings while traveling. If you believe you are being followed, *remain calm, immediately engage your emergency flashers, honk your horn, and drive safely to the police department or other safe location.*

6. Vacation

Vacationing is a time to relax and enjoy time away from the workplace. It is not a time to be careless and caught unprepared.

Inform your local police of the dates you will be away and ask for periodic security checks. If you also have a friend or relative checking your home, inform the police of the person's name, address and phone number. If you return home earlier than expected, notify the police of your return and cancel your vacation security check.

Cancel mail and other routine deliveries, or have a friend or neighbor pick them up daily for you.

Do not leave notes for delivery people at conspicuous locations, thereby announcing your absence.

Store valuables in an alternate safe place while away. This may seem like a considerable inconvenience, but the loss of valuables is an even greater inconvenience.

Leave telephone numbers and/or addresses with friends or relatives as to where you can be reached while on vacation.

7. Work Environment

Many women are in career fields which require them to travel to unfamiliar cities, into the homes of people they do not know, or to and from work at odd times of the day. Your personal safety in these situations is directly related to familiarity and proximity to your office or "home territory." The following precautionary techniques will help you in a risk analysis of your work environment.

A. Timing is important when visiting an unfamiliar location. Prior knowledge of the client is valuable and might be available from company files, from other staff members, or from your personal experience. If your meeting doesn't require a "surprise" visit, it is advisable to call first to gain an assessment of the client's emotional state or attitudes. If the visit can be timed to coincide with daylight hours or the presence of other people, that is the best-case scenario.

B. Assessment is a valuable tool in any profession that requires you to work off-site. When approaching the house, take the following precautions: 1) Take note of all conditions and circumstances as you approach the house; 2) Never stand directly in front of the door as you are waiting for someone to answer the door. It is a good idea to pause a moment and listen to see what is occurring inside before knocking. If anything seems out of order, do not hesitate to immediately leave; 3) Once inside, observe the surroundings and people present. Note objects that might make weapons or barriers should you be attacked. Keep potential emergency exits accessible to you during your visit, and keep your meeting in the public areas of the house such as the living room and dining room. 4) Carry a pager with you. An intentional page is wise by secretly setting off the pager. This alerts the client that you are in direct communication with your office; 5) If a telephone is available, it is advisable to call the office to give notice that you have arrived and of your expected time of departure. Procedures can be established for the office to routinely call back if you are delayed in your departure.

C. Cooperation is essential to avoid conflict which

may result in physical assaults. Many duties in some career fields are perceived by the clients as *enforcement* that sometimes restrict the freedom of the client. Recognize that your duties can be interpreted as negative acts and can induce anger and unannounced violence. Recognize that the client's home and property can be a dangerous environment to you as you carry out your responsibilities.

D. Techniques employed by both men and women should include coping with anger and calming people who become emotional. In some cases, courtesy is a forgotten area of training. A work behavior that carries the stigma of *uncaring* or *mechanical* is not as likely to gain a spirit of cooperative compliance.

Don't Stop Here

Ask your local police department about available crime prevention programs and literature. Your college and local library are also good sources. Most important, don't take chances. Instead, become aware of the possibility we all have of becoming potential victims. Think through your daily routines, always ask yourself, "When I am in this specific situation, this is what I would do if...."

6. Assertion As A Defense Skill

There are many forms of self-defense that are helpful in increasing your determination to fight back against assault and in gaining the confidence to do so. Many rapists and assailants will be frightened away by a

*vigorous show of opposition, even if your
skills are less than perfect.*[1]

Nonverbal Behaviors

Communication experts agree: Well over fifty
percent (50%) of communication originates from body
language, or nonverbal behavior. A person communicates
even when remaining absolutely silent. The ability to
accurately read and send nonverbal messages can affect
the outcome of assaulting or threatening situations.

Phrases such as "walking tall," "with her head
hanging," "standing proud" and "shifty eyes" all bring to
mind mental pictures which tell us something about a
person. Ask a child if he is responsible for a particular
misdeed, and nonverbals such as avoiding eye contact will
tell more about the truth than what the child says.

> *A person's posture and body movement can speak
> volumes about her feelings, self-image and energy
> level. The movement of the head, arms, hands, legs
> and feet can be very revealing. A person wanting to
> terminate a conversation, for instance, may stretch
> her legs, bob her foot, straighten the papers on the
> desk, close her briefcase, and/or sit in an upright
> position in preparation for leaving.*[2]

Some criminals may key in on nonverbal messages
and select targets based somewhat upon these nonverbals.
The victims selected are thought to be easy targets because
of the nonverbals they display.

---

[1]Ellen Ellen and Laura Davis, *The Courage to Heal, A
Guide for Women Survivors of Child Sexual Abuse* (Harper and
Rowe, 1988), p. 221.

[2]Robert Bolton, Ph.D., *People Skills* (Prentice-Hall Inc.,
1979), p. 83.

Imagine two women walking down the street, both the same size, age and sex. Place yourself in the role of the criminal watching the potential victim. Potential victim Number One looks down and directly to the front, scuffs her feet, and walks slowly. Her hands and arms hang motionless at her sides. Her shoulders slouch. Potential victim Number Two holds her head erect, looks around constantly, and walks at a brisk pace. Her shoulders are back and her arms swing in time with her gait.

Which victim do you think will be the easiest target? Number One, of course. You can gain an enhanced awareness of you own body language by consciously noting how you present yourself physically to others.

A victim is not responsible for her own assault because of sending improper "victim like" nonverbals, but nonverbals do play a part in whether you are selected as a victim and must be considered.

If we are perceptive to the messages, body language tells us a lot about other people and tells other people a lot about ourselves. Richard Bolton has identified six sources which telegraph a person's emotions. The six sources originate from two "channels," the *auditory* channel and the *visual* channel:

The *auditory* channel includes (1) specific words that are spoken, (2) the sound of the voice, and (3) the rapidity of speech and frequency and length of pauses.

The *visual* channel includes (1) facial expression, (2) posture, and (3) gestures.

By improving your skill in reading and sending nonverbals you can more accurately read another person's nonverbals. Bolton also explains five guidelines which are helpful in understanding body language:

1. Focus attention on the cues that are thought to be most helpful.

2. Try to see each of these nonverbals in their proper context.

3. Notice incongruities.
4. Heighten your awareness of personal feelings.
5. Reflect your understanding back to the other for confirmation or correction.[3]

Submissive, Assertive, and Aggressive Behaviors

We constantly display behaviors during our waking hours. It is as impossible for people to not display behaviors as it would be for the sun not to emit heat and light. Behaviors can be categorized for purposes of discussion and examination of our personal behaviors and observation of the behavior of others.

To label or categorize a behavior is not to label or categorize the person who exhibits that behavior. Our behaviors change depending upon where we are, who we are with, and what societal role we happen to be playing.

Think of a continuum of behaviors with submissive behaviors on the left, and aggressive behaviors on the right.

SUBMISSIVE   ASSERTIVE   AGGRESSIVE

Assertive behaviors are found in the center of this continuum. Assertive behaviors are usually most appropriate for preventing and coping in rape situations, although there are times when aggressive or submissive behaviors might make good sense in rape situations.

The movies and television often portray either submissive or aggressive behaviors in selected characters. One television sitcom character who was portrayed as very submissive was Edith Bunker from the series *All in the*

---

[3]Op. Cit., pp. 80-81.

Family. Other submissive TV personalities were Barnie Fife, Gilligan, and more recently Ergel. These characters are set up in the show to be laughed at. We often laugh because we observe some of our own behaviors in these characters.

Aggressive behaviors are also frequently displayed in the movies and on TV. Dirty Harry, Kung Fu, and the Terminator are all aggressive and sometimes violent roles. We usually stand in awe of these characters and are amazed at their collective command of situations and seeming invincibility.

Submissive behaviors normally are viewed as having a lack of self-respect and not protecting personal rights. Submissive behaviors will not clearly express personal needs, honest feelings, values or concerns. Other people are likely to violate the rights of submissive people. As discussed earlier, submissive people may be selected more frequently as victims.

Aggressive behaviors normally are viewed as expressing feelings, needs, and ideas at the expense of others through loud, abusive, rude or sarcastic communication. Aggressive people tend to overpower other people with their behaviors.

Assertive behaviors are more commonly observed to use communication to maintain self-respect and to defend personal rights. Assertive people will defend their personal "space." Assertive communication gains a higher degree of voluntary compliance than does submissive or aggressive behavior. Assertive behaviors are less likely to escalate the violence of conflict situations.

Assume that you are observing the following scene in a restaurant. A gentleman is seated in the no-smoking section when a middle aged woman is seated at the table next to him. After a few minutes the man takes out a cigarette and "lights up." The smoke drifts directly into the face of the woman, who is well aware that she has requested and been seated in a no-smoking section.

If the woman responds with submissive behaviors

she will do nothing about the obvious infringement upon her rights and expectations. Should the woman respond with aggressive behaviors, the response might include forcing the man's cigarette into his coffee, or dumping her jello into his lap without warning. An assertive approach, however, might accomplish the objective, and protect the rights of everyone. The woman might say, "Excuse me, are you aware that we are seated in a non-smoking section?" She might then add, "The smoke from your cigarette is causing me great difficulty in breathing and I would appreciate it if you would refrain until I leave."

Consider yourself. Where do you fall on this continuum of behavior as it relates to verbals and nonverbals? If you're not sure, it often helps to ask your friends their perception of your behaviors. It is also helpful to observe others, with the continuum of behaviors in mind.

Here is a common list of "victim behaviors," followed by alternative "nonverbal" and "assertive behaviors." This listing of behaviors was drawn from the book *Safe in the Streets,* by Sandra J. Merwin.

Victim Behavior	Nonverbal	Assertive Behavior
head down eyes down	Eye Contact	look directly at aggressor, alert watchful
shoulders slumped held tight, compacting the body	Body Posture	erect, weight evenly distributed
hands at side, held tight	Gestures	stop or halt gesturing, defensive, fighting position
blank, frightened, closed, timid	Facial Expression	direct, determined, concentrated

Victim Behavior	Nonverbal	Assertive Behavior
squeaky, whispering, pleading, whining	Voice, Tone	well-modulated, concentrated
hesitation, uncertainty	Timing	quick, reactive, spontaneous
apologetic, "I'm sorry"	Content	direct, "Stop," "Leave me alone," "Take your hands off of me."
exaggerated, too long or short	Stride, Movement	medium stride, natural, balanced
lift and place foot	Foot Movement	heel to toe movement
cross movement, right shoulder moving with hip	Torso Movement	right arm moves with left leg, left arm moves with right leg
legs and arms appear to move separately from the body[4]	Totality	arms, legs and body move as one

Victims may be perceived by criminals as "helpless" or "easy marks." Victim-like behaviors may augment this perception by the criminal.

The "Five C's" of Assertive Behavior

It is helpful to think of the "Five C's" of assertive behavior:

1. *Control* is a key factor in maintaining assertive behaviors. Control cannot be taught; it is acquired

---

[4]Sandra J. Merwin, *Safe in the Streets, Don't Be a Victim* (The Book Peddlers, 1982), p. 30.

through experience and practice. Control denotes maintenance of order in situations and keeping a calm disposition during tense and volatile situations.

2. *Courtesy* can be the key in communicating assertive behaviors. Many times the obvious is overlooked in terms of courtesy. A warm and friendly smile, hand shake, positive greeting or genuine openness all denote courtesy and can serve to keep conflict from escalating and possibly keep a person from movement on the continuum towards aggressive behavior.

3. *Communication* is vital to maintenance of assertive behavior. Non-communication could be perceived by others to be either aggressive or submissive behavior. A key to communication is possession of effective active listening skills. Communication, of course, involves both verbal and non-verbal communication and the sending of proper verbal and non-verbal messages which are in agreement with one another.

4. *Cooperation* denotes the mutual-gains theory of negotiation and bargaining. There is little argument that more can be gained through cooperation than through conflict.

5. *Concentration* involves the channeling of the thought process upon the tasks at hand. A person can waiver from the assertive behavior portion of the continuum without concentration. Concentration, like control, cannot be taught. It is gained through experience and practice.

Conflict

Conflict and the potential for conflict exist in every

aspect of society today. Conflict is commonly thought of as a state of disagreement and disharmony bringing to mind such terms as belligerency, hostility, clash, difficulty, dissension, and friction.

Conflict has the potential to escalate and de-escalate depending on many factors. Conflict usually occurs when two divergent persons or groups interact having differing goals, objectives, or immediate needs. Stress and emotion play a large role in how people in conflict are able to resolve their differences.

Two basic reactions to stress and conflict that exist in both the lower and higher animal forms are "fight or flight." Manuel Smith, in his book, *When I Say No, I Feel Guilty,* describes a third reaction to stress and conflict:

> *Although we have fight and flight in common with the lower animals,... what distinguishes us from the other species is our great new verbal and problem-solving brain.... this verbal communication and problem solving ability is the key survival difference....* [5]

Possessing good communication and interpersonal skills will aid those in conflict to resolve that conflict with a minimal potential for escalation. The cost of conflict can be tremendous. Conflict can result in hard feelings, dislike, wasted energies, hatred, or physical assault and the loss of life.

Since conflict is emotionally based, rational thinking often does not play a significant role in the outcome. The person who is able to effectively control conflict is the one who possesses good verbal and non-verbal skills and uses these skills to persuade or negotiate a successful resolution.

---

[5]Manuel J. Smith, Ph.D., *When I Say No, I Feel Guilty* (Bantam Books, 1980), pp. 5-6.

In *The Gentle Art of Verbal Self-Defense,* Suzette Haden Elgin says,

> *Your goal is to keep the level of tension low, to keep your attacker from panicking -- a major danger, however strange it may seem -- and to win time. Be as absolutely neutral as you possibly can.... In the hands of an expert, this will work. That is why experts are sent to negotiate with persons who have shut themselves up in buildings with hostages at gunpoint.... In a beginner's hands it may fail, but it is worth a try.[6]*

Power

The concept of power is germane to discussion of physical assault for several reasons. After all, if the attacker was not in a power position, the attack could not be successful. Power comes from a person's ability to "do something" and has nothing to do with right or authority to complete a particular act or deed.

Power can be possessed by anyone for any reason. A terrorist wields a tremendous amount of power, usually by taking hostages, committing violent acts or making threats.

From another vantage point, an understanding of power can be gained by the idea of being powerless. People quickly realize when they are powerless. A rape victim can be powerless to stop her attacker. Abused family members feel powerless to stop destructive behaviors by other family members. Persons who are dependent on drugs or alcohol feel powerless to change their situation. Many managers feel powerless to significantly impact the course of their organizations.

Power does not necessarily denote physical power.

---

[6]Suzette Haden-Elgin, *The Gentle Art of Verbal Self-Defense* (Prentice-Hall, 1980), p. 305.

An attacker gains a power advantage through several methods, some of which are:

1.   *Intimidation* is often used by an attacker to gain a power advantage. Behaviors from the aggressive end of the behavior continuum will serve to frighten and intimidate the victim. The attacker may have some expectations in terms of victim reactions. (Review chapter 7 about verbal and nonverbal alternatives, particularly "insane verbals and nonverbals.")

2.   *Tactical advantage* is achieved by the attacker when the victim is surprised or shocked. The attacker may "come from nowhere," or "was just there." Victim powers of observation will play a key role in the attackers ability to achieve tactical advantage through surprise. Tactical advantage can also be achieved by selecting a location for the attack that offers concealment and generally a minimal opportunity for detection of the crime by others. Most criminals have a primary goal of "not being caught" during commission of the crime. Many criminals who are caught and arrested for commission of a crime are primarily remorseful for having been caught. They feel they have made an error in not planning or executing the crime properly.

3.   *Perception of physical strength* can give an extreme power advantage to the attacker. Many defensive tactics skills that utilize speed and "technique" can overcome elements of physical strength by the attacker. Chapter 8 discusses some elements of defensive tactics techniques that are useful in attack situations.

4.   *Actual or threatened use of a weapon* offers an

immediate power advantage to the attacker. When the attacker indicates that he or she is in possession of a weapon, it is wise to believe them until it is proven otherwise. Many gas stations and convenience stores are robbed by people who say they have a gun, when it may only be their finger poking the inner lining of a pocket. The wise cashier believes the robber and does not challenge the apparent power position of the robber. Physical techniques that are designed to "disarm" the attacker require hundreds of hours of practice. The decision to attempt to disarm an attacker is a serious one that may have grave consequences for you.

5. *Expected victim reaction.* The attacker may have an expected victim reaction in mind before the attack. Assertive or aggressive behaviors by the victim may counteract the power balance.

Assertion can be a valuable defense tool. Assertion is a skill that can be improved with practice and experience. Assertion can destroy the expected reaction the attacker may have of you and affect the power balance in your favor.

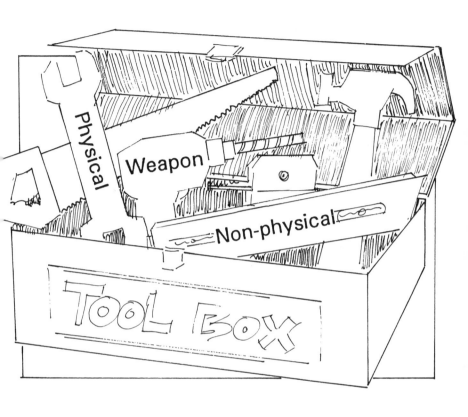

7. Defensive Tactics Alternatives

Usually the ability to say no firmly and to move out of a threatening situation is enough to keep you safe. But sometimes an assailant will not be repelled by words alone.

83

*Then you need to use additional
self-defense skill to keep you
from further violation--shouting,
yelling, kicking, hitting and
making use of your wits and
intuition.*[1]

Tactics are skills to gain a particular goal. In this case our goal is self-defense from assault and potential assault situations. *Alternatives* are various courses of action and reaction to take when facing a threatening situation. To be *defensive* means that force is applied reasonably and in proportion to the amount of force that is applied to you. The overall goal is to possess many alternatives through pre-planning and practice, so that the proper alternatives can be used at the appropriate time. When alternatives are limited, the chances for survival diminish. When alternatives are broad, survival opportunities increase.

Each student of defensive tactics begins this study from a different starting point. Each has her own level of skill and knowledge about defensive tactics. But whatever your preparation level now, it is safe to say that you can improve your current level of preparation.

No defensive tactics instructor or program can guarantee success. If they do make this promise, they are not to be trusted. There are no guarantees that any amount of preparation will result in successful self-defense. However, proper mental and physical conditioning can decrease the chances of becoming a victim. The objective of learning more about defensive alternatives is to possess many "tools" to be used in assault situations.

---

[1]Ellen Bass and Laura Davis, *The Courage to Heal, A Guide for Women Survivors of Child Sexual Abuse* (Harper & Row, 1988), p. 221.

There are three broad categories of alternatives for use in confrontational situations: weapon alternatives, physical alternatives, and non-physical alternatives. We will discuss each category separately, but you should understand that using alternatives from each of the three categories in combination is usually most successful, depending on the situation you are in.

There are an infinite number and combinations of weapon, physical, and non-physical techniques. We cannot possibly cover them all. Our goal is to build a framework of knowledge and awareness from which you will be able to build a repertoire of skills.

When To Use Force

Any discussion of techniques that involve applying physical force against another human being must first talk about when to use force. One would not consider for a moment a suggestion that newly trained student drivers should only receive instruction in "how to drive an automobile" (the mechanics of driving) without also receiving extensive instruction in the "rules of the road" (traffic laws).

In the same way, there are potential civil and criminal implications whenever force is used against another person, either with or without a weapon. The "self-defense" legal defense is generally held by courts to be valid if the person using force honestly believes he or she is in danger of death or great bodily harm, and that it is necessary to act as he or she did in order to save himself.

The legal requirements do change from county to county and state to state. Therefore, we advise you to consult with legal authorities in your area for specific information about the use of force.

It may be helpful to think of the three types of alternatives as a continuum with non-physical alternatives on the extreme left, physical alternatives in the center, and weapon alternatives on the far right of the continuum. As you move from the left to the right, the potential for serious injury or death to the receiver of the techniques increases. It is unlikely that someone could be physically injured by a non-physical alternative, but would likely be injured if you were to use a weapon alternative.

Alternatives Continuum

Non-Physical	Physical	Weapon

Take care when selecting a technique from one of the three alternatives to ensure that the type of techniques employed are justified and fit the situation. And recognize that we cannot tell you when to use or not use force. You alone must make that decision, and ultimately will be held accountable for its use.

Weapons Alternatives

There are two categories of weapons: instruments that are fashioned and intended for use as weapons; and items in your surroundings that can be used as weapons, although intended for some other purpose.

A weapon will not always improve your chances of survival in an assault situation. Having a weapon sometimes creates a false sense of security for the user. Remember, if a weapon is available to you, the same weapon is also available to your attacker. Most items suggested for use as weapons are not likely to be available when needed. No matter what weapon you carry, you may still not be prepared for the surprise attack. Even if you are prepared, remember your intended weapon can be taken away and used against you by an attacker. Inherent in the use of any weapon is a responsibility by the user to know how and when to use it, and that use must be legally justified.

The two most common "weapons" are guns and knives. Both of these weapons are potentially deadly and have safety risks to the user. Handguns are commonly purchased to "protect the home." "One very common means of coping with fear is owning a gun... slightly over half of all Americans own guns."[2]

Ironically, there is a much greater likelihood of a family member being injured from a handgun accident in the home, than there is from being the victim of a crime in the home.

> But the great bulk of expert opinion is that owning a gun undermines rather than increases safety: whatever deterrence of burglars or rapists might occur is more than offset by other factors... first come suicides... then come the accidental shootings, many by klutzes who never bother to learn how to handle their weapons. More heartbreaking are the frequent incidents of children picking up their parents' guns... police commonly estimate that if a household gun is ever used at all, it is six times as likely to be fired at a member of the family or a friend as at an intruder.[3]

Another irony is that most illegal handguns on the streets are stolen from homes during burglaries! Many jurisdictions have local and state laws that control the carrying of handguns and other dangerous weapons. These laws should be researched and strictly adhered to when considering the purchase or carrying of guns or knives for *any* purpose.

---

[2]*The Figgie Report on Fear of Crime: America Afraid Part I* (Research & Forecasts, Inc., 1980), p. 23.

[3]George J. Church, "The Other Arms Race," *Time*, February 6, 1989, p. 20.

Potential Weapons

Some potential "environmental weapons" are listed below. These weapons have the advantage of availability. The disadvantage is their limited effectiveness because of design. Even though these environmental weapons are not intended for use as weapons, for purposes of civil and criminal liability, they can be treated the same as an actual weapon.

* *Keys:* Keys can be held in the hand on the way to and from your car, apartment or home. The keys can be used as a poking, scratching, or gouging weapon. Take care to have the proper key in hand, have it held properly so that it will insert into the lock, and know which way the lock turns in order to lock or unlock the door.

* *Hairbrush:* The hairbrush is commonly found in purses and in the home. This item could be a useful striking weapon for self-defense.

* *Comb:* The comb is often close at hand and might be used as a poking or gouging weapon.

* *Book:* Books can be used for striking, or thrown into the attacker's face for a momentary shock effect in order to select another alternative.

* *Umbrella:* Although not as commonly available as other items mentioned here, the umbrella is potentially a better self-defense weapon. The length and design of the umbrella affords a wider range of striking, poking or pushing possibilities.

* *Rings:* The success of this item may depend on how big your ring is. Some rings are good for gouging or grinding.

* **Nail file:** The nail file is close to a knife in design and can offer some of the same application. Remember that any weapon available to you may be available to your attacker.

* **Plastic squirt container filled with lemon juice:** Lemon juice, when squirted into your attacker's facial area, can cause momentary stinging of the eyes. Keep this item near your front door just in case.

* **Chemicals:** Other household chemicals could be used as potential weapons of self-defense. Caution should be used as many household chemicals can cause permanent injury or even death. The use of chemicals would most likely be used in last resort situations.

* **Hair spray:** Direct the hair spray toward your attackers face to cause irritation of the eyes.

* **Dirt or sand:** If dirt or sand is available, it too can be directed toward the face of the attacker, much as is portrayed in the western movies.

* **Ink pen or pencil:** Use these in self-defense encounters for jabbing the attacker.

* **Lapel stick-pins:** This item is not as common as it once was, but if available, could be used to poke or gouge the attacker.

Last Resort Techniques

Use last resort techniques only when you believe there are no other options for survival. When you sincerely believe your life or physical safety is jeopardized, any available object such as a chair, lamp, or piece of wood may be used as a weapon.

Last resort techniques can result in serious, permanent injury or death. Remember: There are legal implications whenever force is used, either with or without a weapon. We cannot tell you when to use or not use force. You alone must make that decision, and ultimately will be held accountable for its use.

Physical Alternatives

Physical alternatives are those techniques that require expenditure of physical energy in order to complete. "Of course, there will always be situations in which you can't fight back successfully, or in which you judge it more dangerous to do so. But if you have basic self-defense training, if you feel powerful and entitled, you can protect yourself much more of the time."[4]

The degree of success for any physical alternative depends upon many factors. Important considerations to remember when employing any physical alternative are: your personal physical capabilities and limitations; your degree of competence in execution of a particular technique; your mental and attitude preparation; and the effectiveness of the technique upon the attacker.

Physical alternatives are limited only by your imagination. Here are a few to consider:

1. *Avoidance strategies:* The degree of success of this physical alternative is tied closely to your powers of observation discussed in a previous chapter. In order to avoid potential danger you must first be able to observe and recognize that danger. One of the barriers to successful avoidance is the "rushed" atmosphere that exists in everyday life, coupled with a certain reluctance to ask for help from others.

---

[4]Op. cit., p. 221.

For example, assume that you are leaving a large shopping center after dark and notice a van parked next to your vehicle. Since there are no other vehicles near yours or the strange van, you have some choices and options open to you. The easiest choice is to merely walk to your car and leave as you otherwise would. If you have recognized a potential for danger, you might choose to ask a bagger or store manager to accompany you to your car. There are many other options for you in this situation that could be categorized as avoidance strategies. The police could be summoned to investigate the van. If that seems too drastic considering the situation, you might push a shopping cart out to your car for use as a barrier between you and any potential attackers.

2. *Running away:* This alternative is also linked closely to observation skills -- because it is one thing to be able to run, but quite another to know where to run. It is important to periodically look about for potential "safe areas" in case of an assault.

    Assume that you are walking down a city street one evening and have just passed several homes. All the homes are completely dark except one where a gentleman is sitting in the living room reading the newspaper. Just as you pass this home you are faced with a mugger and you choose to run away. If you have been observant, the safe direction to flee is to the house that you just passed. If you have not been observant, you might run the opposite direction which may not offer any immediate safe place.

    Physical conditioning is a key component of this alternative. A person who tires when climbing one flight of stairs at work may not run far before collapsing in trying to escape from an assailant.

Other factors to be considered when choosing to run are the type of footwear and whether clothing is tight or loose fitting. It is fortunate that business attire and tennis shoes are now acceptable for both men and women.

3.   *Unexpected non-verbals:* Non-verbals include all body messages other than the spoken word. The intent of using unexpected non-verbals is to possibly confuse the attacker with a response that he or she did not expect. This alternative alone may have limited impact toward the goal of self-defense. However, if used to "buy time" for selection of other alternatives, it may be useful.

Some examples of unexpected non-verbals are hitting yourself, barking like a dog, faking insanity, choking, inducing vomiting, and so on. These behaviors again may interrupt the expected response the attacker has for the situation, or give some time for selection of other alternatives. This alternative alone may not offer a tremendous advantage to you and should be considered in conjunction with other tactics.

4.   *Muscle relaxation:* This response seeks to invoke a similar response in your attacker. Your relaxation could cause the attacker to momentarily loosen the grip or hold being applied. Going completely limp and becoming a dead weight can make it difficult for anyone to move you to another location or into a vehicle.

A close cousin to muscle relaxation is to pretend to completely comply with your attacker's initial physical movements. For example, if your attacker begins to pull you by the arm, running into the direction of that pull can be a proper defensive response. This is discussed at length in chapter 8 which describes the "push-pull" concept.

5   *Fighting back:* Unfortunately, with this technique there are seldom any fair rules, referees or umpires. You will be judged for your actions through later analysis by your peers, courts and attorneys. Choosing this alternative indicates that the assault has escalated to the degree where this recourse is necessary.

If you fight back, it is important to have a reasonable degree of proficiency in techniques being applied. Also, if your efforts fail or result in a more violent response from your attacker, switch to another alternative.

This is not an exhaustive list. Many responses are possible through combining weapon and physical alternatives. The decision of which combination of alternatives to use is a personal one. Base your decision on the facts and conditions you believe exist at the time of the incident.

It is important to pre-plan and to develop additional plans should the first one fail. Remain flexible and do not continue one course of action if it proves ineffective. Remember, most actions taken during an assault are the result of split-second decisions made with little or no time to consider all possibilities. The lack of time is the enemy of sound decision-making.

Non-Physical Alternatives

Non-physical alternatives range from saying nothing to screaming frantically. They include quiet, controlled, verbal responses to those of telling, directing, ordering, negotiating, using persuasion and speaking gibberish. In *The Gentle Art of Verbal Self-Defense*, Suzette Haden Elgin gives advise to persons who might be faced with an assaultive encounter: "Your goal is to keep the level of tension low, to keep your attacker from panicking -- a major danger, however strange it may seem -- and to win time. Be absolutely neutral as you possibly can."[5]

Below are a few non-physical alternatives:

1.   **Remain Silent:** Remaining silent in certain situations may be successful in avoiding the conflict altogether. Some assailants may attempt to incite or aggravate a potential victim with challenges or threats. The potential victim who remains quiet, not acknowledging the communication at all, will not contribute to the escalation of the conflict. Remaining silent is not easy to do in highly emotional or tense situations. Remaining silent is often perceived as a sign of weakness. On the contrary, it takes enormous strength to consciously maintain composure in such settings.

2.   **Assertive Verbals:** This defensive alternative is designed to gain voluntary compliance with your commands without the use of physical alternatives. Again, assertiveness is a form of total communication that sends a very clear and concise message to the intended receiver. Assertive persons stand up and protect their own rights, but not at the expense of the rights of others.

    The tone, volume, inflection, and quality of a person's voice are important to the perceived assertiveness of any spoken message. Simple, assertive commands like "Stop," "Leave me alone," and "Take your hands off of me," may elicit compliance with that command. Many of us have been conditioned to respond to similar commands

---

[5]Suzette Haden Elgin, *The Gentle Art of Verbal Self-Defense* (Prentice-Hall, 1980), p. 305.

and again, the attacker may not expect this response from you.

3. **Negotiate:** Negotiation is the art of bargaining, or giving the perception of bargaining, with another person. The perception must be given that something is given up for another concession in return. Negotiation is most commonly associated with the process of collective bargaining labor agreements. Both the "company" and the "employees" participate in a process of give and take until an agreement is reached.

Negotiation is used widely, and successfully, by law enforcement agencies in hostage and barricaded gunman situations. In the law enforcement experience, the longer a situation goes without the need for the use of forceful intervention, the less likely it is that force will be needed to resolve that conflict.

On one occasion, a young woman was successful using negotiation to avoid a sexual assault. This woman was sleeping in her own bedroom one evening when one of her worst fears was realized. She was awakened by a strange man who had broken into her home, intent on rape. This woman chose to negotiate with her attacker. She gave the appearance that "...it doesn't have to be this way." She suggested that she would be willing to meet him at another time and place -- all for the cause of appealing to the attacker's sense of reason to be able to "get what he wanted" without committing a crime. It worked for this young woman. The attacker left without completing the crime he had intended. Negotiation, like all other skills, may require practice in order to achieve any degree of proficiency.

4. **Screaming or yelling:** This has three potential purposes: shocking your attacker, attracting attention to your plight, or inflicting pain into the ear of your attacker. The location of the attack may dictate how successful or unsuccessful you are in attracting the attention of others. Making the attacker think that you are attracting attention may serve the same purpose as actually doing so.

    The shock value of a scream or yell is well known to practitioners of the martial arts. The "kei" (yell) not only shocks the opponent, but helps to focus power into a strike or blow being delivered at the time. This is one example of beginning to think of, and use, the different types of alternatives in conjunction. The scream or yell can also inflict pain and momentary loss of attention of an attacker. If this technique is used, however, a complete course of action to follow would be desired, as screaming alone may not offer total hope of success.

In summary, we have explored three categories of responses to an attack: weapon alternatives, physical alternatives, and non-physical alternatives. It helps to think of these three types of alternatives as a collection of tools. If you possess and know how to use many tools, your chances of survival could increase.

One key to success is to take some time for introspection and self-examination. Determine where your skill and knowledge levels are in each of the three categories. Then it will be possible to seek out resources to build upon existing levels of knowledge and skill. Our chapter devoted to physical techniques will provide a starting point from which to build some additional physical alternatives.

These physical, non-physical and weapon alternatives are best practiced through role-playing in a classroom or by thinking through potential situations in a "what if?" case-by-case thought process. Remember that an alternative unexplored is an alternative not available at the time of confrontation.

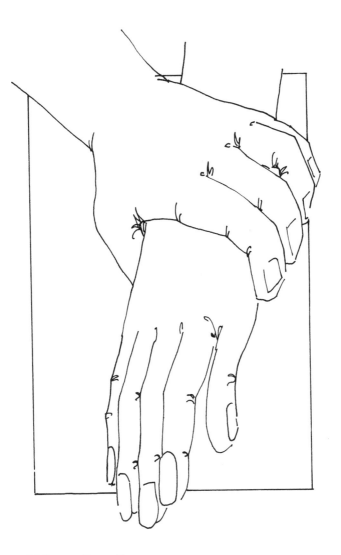

8. *Physical Defense Techniques*

*Those who have no preparation
in self-defense techniques will*

strike out wildly in panic or
seeming panic.[1]

A Team Concept: Exercise + Preparation

Previous chapters have explored the need to learn and practice prevention strategies. Another important component of self-defense is that of physical fitness and physical defense techniques.

There are many reasons to exercise regularly: to increase heart health, improve upper body strength and joint flexibility, to release stress, and to achieve a general feeling of well-being. Another reason is to increase your chances of "winning" when in physical danger due to an assault.

Comparable reasons exist for learning simple self-defense techniques or "moves," of which there are hundreds. Achieving a balance of physical fitness and self-defense skill can improve survival opportunities in physical assault situations.

It is a timeworn story about the muscular bully who kicks sand into the face of the frail "nerd" on the beach. The nerd enrolls in body-building and self-defense programs and returns soon after to settle the score with the bully. This simplistic example illustrates that there is some basis for the nerd's increased chances of surviving the second confrontation because of his exercise and preparation.

A person who has a weapon may have a false sense of security in physical assault situations. You must be equally cautious not to be overconfident because you possess some knowledge and skill in physical defense techniques such as judo, karate, or other martial arts.

It is imperative to have an accurate picture of both the capabilities and limitations that these physical techniques may afford to you. We have a tendency to

---

[1]Bruce Tegner, *Nerve Centers and Pressure Points* (Ventura, California: Thor Publishing Company, 1976), p. 19.

overestimate the value of "hand-to-hand" techniques in any given situation. The ideal approach is to enhance your knowledge of defensive tactics and also to exercise regularly to increase your endurance and strength.

Learning any skill requires practice. The first goal of practice is to learn the skill. The second goal is to master the skill so that it becomes a natural response and therefore useful under stressful conditions.

Imagine you are watching a little league game of tee ball. Danny is playing shortstop for the first time in his life. A fast ground ball is hit to him. He reacts, but much too slowly. The ball travels between his legs into left field. Danny bends over and watches the ball through his legs with an upside down view.

Now let's jump ahead to a championship game ten years later. Danny is again playing shortstop. A hard ground ball is belted at him. Without thinking, Danny dives to the left, snags the sharply hit ball and whips it to first base in one smooth stroke. What key factor has made the difference over these ten years? Practice, practice, and more practice -- thousands of repetitions by Danny in fielding ground balls.

The exposure that you gain in any defensive tactics class gives basic information on how to perform the technique, but the extra effort needed to master the skill must be accomplished outside of the classroom. The level of success you achieve depends solely upon the amount of personal commitment you make. Here are some factors to consider when practicing:

Balance

When performing a defensive technique, your body should be in a balanced position. That is, your weight should be evenly distributed over your feet and legs. Your body should remain balanced as you move, walk, or run. Keeping a balanced posture also sends assertive nonverbal signals to others who might be watching. If you are not balanced, then the technique will lose speed, strength, and effectiveness.

Center of Gravity

A general rule of balance is that the lower you can keep your center of gravity, the better it is for you. Which football player would you prefer to tackle, a five-foot-two, 280 pound torpedo, or a six-foot-four, 130 pound string bean? The difference is in the center of gravity. If you are able to get your opponent off-balance or in a position with a high center of gravity, it can be to your advantage. Judo techniques rely heavily on this principle.

Push-Pull

The push-pull concept is deeply ingrained in defensive tactics. The goal is to use your opponent's body weight and momentum against him. An example of push-*push* is when two rams are literally butting heads as we have often observed in wildlife films.

And example of *pull*-pull is the traditional tug-of-war involving any number of participants and a strong rope. Imagine what would happen in the first example of push-push if one of the rams skillfully stepped aside just prior to impacting the other ram? In the example of pull-pull, what laws of physics would come into play if one of the teams, at a prearranged signal, suddenly let go of the rope?

The concept of push-pull is simple: U*se your opponent's actions to your advantage.* When he pushes, you would pull and not try to interrupt that force and momentum. If your opponent pulls, you would respond with a push or possibly a tripping technique that could use his force or momentum to your advantage.

Example: Imagine a stranger trying to push his way into a door that your are holding closed. When you cannot hold out much longer, merely pull the door open. This may catch your attacker off balance. He may stumble into the doorway for a long enough time to allow you to run past him and out the door to safety.

Conservation of Energy

If your body and mind are both in an extreme state of tension, you will waste vast amounts of physical and emotional energy. Energy can often be conserved through self awareness of breath control and relaxation of unneeded muscles.

Skill Level

A good defensive tactics program will place you under a mild degree of stress. This experience will prepare you for some of the tension caused by being unfamiliar with the techniques, and this is another reason for practice, practice, practice.

A useful model for learning any physical skill is to think of a ten-rung ladder. Consider the first rung as the slowest possible execution of a particular skill and the tenth rung as being full-force execution of that skill. Begin by working on steps one through three of the skill ladder. Only through hours of repetition and instructor guidance should you venture up the skill ladder to the tenth rung. Premature attempts to execute a new skill at full speed can result in failure and personal injury.

Safety

Safety is a primary concern when learning a skill that uses another human being as a practice "dummy." A universal "tapping" signal is used to signal that the person being practiced on is experiencing pain or discomfort which may result in injury. The rule is that the "dummy" will tap anything to signal the other person to immediately release all pressure and stop the technique. It is preferable to tap the student on a part of his or her body, and it is expected that at least two taps in quick succession will be made. It is also allowable for the "dummy" to tap the floor, a wall or himself to signal the stop request. The importance of practicing safety while participating in any form of defensive tactics cannot be overstated. Horseplay will likely result in injuries.

Main Objective of Defensive Tactics

The main objective of defensive tactics in self-defense situations is to throw the attacker off-guard, or to incapacitate him long enough to escape. Your major focus should always be to escape. You are not trying to win a fight.

Caution: We must remind you, there are no guarantees that any technique will work in all situations. As discussed earlier, your physical and psychological makeup contributes to your ability to resist in either a passive or physical sense.

Major Martial Arts Disciplines

Defensive tactics techniques are drawn from a variety of sources including karate, judo, aikido, jujitsu, boxing and wrestling. A major source of these techniques is from the "martial arts" of which there are two primary disciplines -- judo and karate. Techniques and variations of techniques number in the hundreds and are instructed in training clubs around the world. A short description of the two major forms of martial arts may assist in deciding which discipline may suit your purposes, should this type of preparation appeal to you.

Judo

Judo means "gentle way" in Japanese, and was conceived and first instructed in 1882 by Dr. Jigaro Kano in Japan. This martial art was developed from jujitsu minus the techniques that could cause serious injury. Judo relies upon leverage and balance to overcome your opponent, and uses the concept of push-pull to use the opponent's body weight and momentum to your advantage. Judo is an art that concentrates on both physical and mental conditioning.

Karate

Karate means "empty fist" in Japanese. Unlike judo, karate relies upon hand- and foot-strikes to the opponent. It was the only form of self defense for unarmed farmers and villagers against armed warriors on the island of Okinawa in the 17th century. Karate was introduced in Japan in the 1920s and, after WWII, soldiers returning from the Orient brought karate to the United States.

Karate involves hand- foot- and elbow-strikes against the opponent. The targets of these blows are at vital target areas of the opponent. The result of a full speed strike can be permanent injury or death.

Choosing a Course of Action

Proficiency in any form of the martial arts requires hard work, study and many hours of concentrated repetition. The following factors need to be considered when choosing the study of any defensive tactics discipline:

1. *Physical Fitness:* If you are a heavy smoker or out of shape, recognize your limitations and how they will affect successful execution of a defensive tactic technique. Some techniques do not require extraordinary strength or vast time commitments. Do not completely avoid study of defensive tactics alternatives because you feel you are "out of shape."

2. *Familiarity With Techniques:* You must practice your defensive tactics techniques to the point that your response is automatic or "second nature." It is not likely that a technique will be effective against an assailant unless it can be executed with speed, accuracy and automatic response.

3. **Apparel:** How you are dressed will affect your freedom of movement. High heels or tight-fitting clothes will restrict your ability to defend yourself. Fortunately, it is now acceptable to wear running or jogging shoes to and from work and at lunch hours. This type of footwear can be to your advantage in potential assault situations. If you participate in formal defensive tactics training, you will be required to wear loose-fitting clothes to afford freedom of movement. Remember that performing defensive techniques in "street clothes" will be more difficult.

4. **Control:** How would you rate your ability to stay calm? Many instructors feel this type of control cannot be taught. We believe that self-control and the ability to remain calm in a confrontation can be enhanced through training that focuses on preparing in advance for the unexpected.

Combining Strategies

During the training of recruit officers in police academies, a major instructional strategy is to provide training and "need to know" information through lectures, hands-on practice sessions, scenarios, and other techniques. The goal is to provide officers with passive skills and physical skills to react safely, efficiently and effectively to confrontations. Until tested in the real world, it is unknown with certainty how the officer will react in an emergency. Training serves as a foundation to prepare for unexpected confrontations. Without actual experience in managing the attack/rape confrontation, preventative training is your only realistic alternative.

Risk Zones of the Body

When learning defensive tactics, it is important to consider information about the risk zones of the human body so you can know:

1. The effects your strikes and punches can cause to the person you strike.
2. The effects the same strikes and punches can have on you if you are the victim.

The human body consists of three risk zones: above the shoulder, abdomen, and the arms and legs (also called the four extremities). The risk zones need to be viewed from two distinct perspectives. First, how they can be used as target areas in an opponent, and what likely injuries could result. Second, how they are points of vulnerability and how you can protect yourself in a physical attack. A brief overview of each of the risk zones follows:

1. The Area Above the Shoulders
The head houses the brain, the organ that controls all bodily functions. A sharp blow to the head can cause loss of hearing, loss of eyesight, temporary or permanent paralysis, can interrupt cardio-pulmonary function, and can cause death.

The head also contains the eyes. Striking the eye can cause temporary or permanent blindness, or merely cause tearing which diminishes a person's ability to see and sometimes think clearly. Severe gouging of the eye can actually displace the eyeball from its socket.

The nose is made of cartilage and is easily broken. A person who is struck on the nose can lose mental control and will tend to focus attention on the injury. Bleeding is common when the nose is injured. The nose is also one of two orifices through which life-giving air is obtained. Any restriction of the nasal passages, either by blockage or intentional restriction, can be life-threatening should the mouth also be blocked. Contrary to popular belief, the nose cannot be pushed into the brain causing death. However, medical shock resulting from the blow can be life-threatening under certain conditions.

The jaw is another sensitive area of the head. The

jaw is easily broken, causing great pain. The jaw also houses teeth which can be knocked loose or out with a strike to the jaw area. A person with a "glass jaw" is one who is susceptible to losing consciousness when struck in the jaw. This occurs when the jaw is forced back by the blow. The head and neck also snap back, causing a temporary interruption in blood flow to the brain, resulting in the loss of consciousness.

The ears can be easily damaged by poking a narrow object into them. Damage can also occur if you cup your hands and strike each side of the head over the ears. This can break the eardrums and result in a hearing loss.

The neck is supported by the cervical vertebra located at the back of the neck. A sharp blow or a severe "snapping back" of the neck can paralyse the body. The neck also contains the windpipe through which air passes to the lungs. The windpipe is made of cartilage and is not resilient. Think of the cardboard tube inside a roll of paper towels. If the roll is crushed, the tube does not regain its original shape. Much the same properties are true of the windpipe.

Trauma to the muscles surrounding the windpipe can cause swelling and pressure which threatens air passage through the windpipe. The carotid arteries pass along each side of the windpipe toward the front part of the neck and supply oxygen-rich blood to the brain. Any pinching-off of these arteries will cause unconsciousness in a few seconds, and brain damage or death in a few minutes.

2. The Abdomen

The chest and upper abdomen house many vital organs including the heart, liver, kidneys, and lungs. Police officer are trained to shoot into this "center mass" area, since a wound here is very likely to stop the suspect's threatening behavior. To a lesser degree, any blows to the floating ribs can cause bruising or breakage. Not only is this painful, but there is danger that a broken rib can

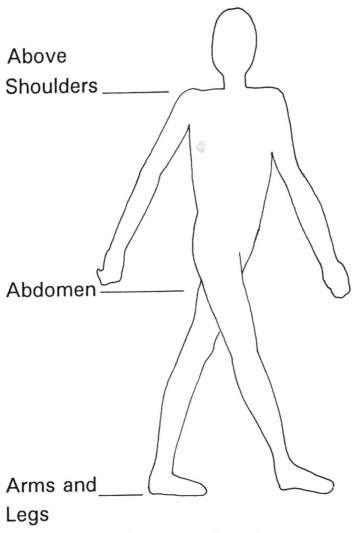

Above Shoulders _____

Abdomen _____

Arms and ____ **Legs**

Risk zones of the body

puncture one of the lungs.

Blows or jabs to the solar plexus are extremely painful and can "knock the wind out" of a person by expelling air from the lungs. The common reaction is to "double up" in an attempt to refill the lungs. A person who is struggling for air is physical vulnerable.

The frontal groin area of men is highly sensitive because of the testicles. Striking or grabbing the testicles can cause severe pain and temporary immobilization of that person. Permanent damage can occur. A myth exists that a strike to the groin area produces automatic and complete incapacitation. There is no guarantee that incapacitation will occur with such a strike to the groin.

3. Arms and Legs (Four Extremities)

The arms and legs are the least vital in terms of the potential for permanent or life-threatening injuries. They are, however, key to many defensive tactics techniques. Joint counter-pressure, pain-compliance and loss of support techniques can be very effective. Of particular interest are the shins and forearms where nerves run close to the surface or where there is little or no fat or muscle covering the bone. Think of the arms and legs as focal points during a confrontation, for they are the most likely "personal weapons" the attacker will use.

Defensive Tactics Perspective

Preparing for personal protection requires many individual decisions. Choosing to learn about physical defensive tactics techniques is but one of those decisions. When weighing the importance of defensive tactics techniques remember that your best investment of time and effort is in practicing preventive strategies. This lesson has been clearly learned in other areas such as fire prevention, crime prevention and loss prevention. Choosing to study defensive tactics to the exclusion of preventive strategies could be an error.

9. Acquaintance Assaults

If you are a woman, your risk of being raped by someone you know is four times greater than your risk of being raped by a stranger.[1]

You are more likely to be sexually assaulted by someone you know than by a stranger. Estimates of the frequency of acquaintance rapes vary depending on the population and type of statistical survey being conducted. These estimates range from more than fifty percent (50%) to as many as ninety percent (90%) of all reported sexual assaults being committed by a person who is at a minimum "acquainted" with the victim.[2]

Acquaintance assaults are commonly referred to as "date rapes," but also include a large percentage of sexual assaults committed by family members, members of the same household, or true acquaintances.

The victims of rape, whether by an acquaintance or a stranger, suffer similar physical and emotional trauma. In a date rape both the victim and the assailant have initially chosen to be together. The risk of date rape is diminished only by the degree of mutual trust, respect, and knowledge within the relationship. Since mutual trust and respect are usually built over time, the risks of becoming the victim of a date rape may be higher during new relationships. Elements of force, intimidation and fear are factors in date rape, as they are in other forms of rape.

In *Against our Will, Men, Women, and Rape,* Susan Brownmiller discusses some of the elements of force:

---

[1]Robin Warshaw, *I Never Called It Rape* (Harper and Rowe, 1988), p. 11.

[2]Mary P. Koss, Thomas E. Dinero, Cynthia A. Seibel, "Stranger and Acquaintance Rape, Are there Differences in the Victims Experience?" *Psychology of Women Quarterly,* 1988, Vol. 12, p. 7.

Date rapes and rapes by men who have had prior relationships with their victims also contain elements of coercive authority and that mitigates against decisive resistance. Here, the "authority" takes the form of expected behavior. In a dating situation an aggressor may press his advantage to the point where pleasantness quickly turns to unpleasantness and more than the woman bargained for....[3]

As discussed in earlier chapters, the attacker may have preconceived expectations of the victim's response during the initial stages of this type of an assault. Brownmiller goes on to say:

...yet social propriety and the strictures of conventional female behavior that dictate politeness and femininity demand that the female gracefully endure, or wriggle away if she can, but a direct confrontation falls outside of the norms.[4]

Preventive strategies intended to counteract the elements of coercion and expected responses will be discussed later in the chapter.

Factors Affecting Acquaintance Assaults

Several factors play instrumental roles in acquaintance assaults. *Expectations and attitudes* about sex vary from person to person and are based upon many factors too numerous to mention. The origin of perceptions about fear and danger were explored in chapter two. The same building blocks exist for perceptions, attitudes, and expectations about sexual matters. The attitudes and

---

[3]Susan Brownmiller, *Against Our Will, Men, Women and Rape* (Bantam Books, 1986), p. 285.

[4]Ibid., p. 284.

expectations of both the victim and the perpetrator affect the outcome of acquaintance assaults.

It is difficult to believe, but still true, that some people possess attitudes that view the female half of a date as "owing" after an evening out. This "owing" attitude may lay the ground work for an acquaintance assault. Some assailants actually will "stalk" their victims at singles bars, large public parties or similar places.

Our purpose is not to attempt to understand these attitudes and beliefs, but only to be aware that they exist. On a more radical note, it is also difficult to believe that a person could "justify" walking into a party store, then robbing and murdering the store clerk. Paranoia is not the purpose, only acceptance that many different types of people make up this society, and that a very small percentage of them are potentially dangerous.

It may be helpful to remind young men that it is their responsibility to realize that "no" does mean no, and that the consequences of their actions could be criminal prosecution for violation of a sexual assault law.

Communication or the lack of communication may set into play certain misunderstandings about how a date is to end. Robin Warshaw writes in *I Never Called It Rape,*

> *Miscommunication contributes to the factual and perceptual fogs that cloud acquaintance rape incidents. This miscommunication may occur because men and women often interpret behavior cues and can direct conversation differently. In general, men give a more sexual reading to behavior and conversation than women do.*[5]

Women need to use their perceptual abilities to tune into the signals they receive and send that have the

---

[5]Op. Cit., p. 41.

potential to create an acquaintance assault environment. Recognize the sexual innuendoes or a conversational emphasis on sexual topics. Use your assertive skills to communicate that you feel uncomfortable with that type of talk.

It can also be useful to communicate clearly your sexual values and expectations. Tell your date that the second, third, or fourth date is too early for sexual involvement. Tell your date that a willingness to kiss does not give him license to "go farther." Tell your date that "no means no." Draw him out on his expectations about sex. Does he believe that "teases get what they deserve"? Does he subscribe to the attitude that women "owe" their dates sex in certain circumstances?

The setting can also play an important role in acquaintance assaults. Often the victim has some control over the setting for the date. It may be beneficial to keep meetings or dates in public places, if possible. Shirley Pettier and Janet Torge offer advice on this point in *A Book About Sexual Assault:* "If you are seeing someone you barely know, arrange to meet him in a restaurant, a bar, or other public place. This will reduce your fears and avoid a potentially uncomfortable situation."[6]

Alcohol and drug use by the victim can diminish her ability to protect herself. Physical and mental powers of reasoning are affected by drugs and alcohol. Many victims of date rape report "passing out" due to excessive alcohol consumption. They later wake up in bed with a man and literally have no recollection of what may have happened.

Alcohol and drug use by the assailant will likewise affect his behaviors. Keen observations should be made for any indications of behavior changes due to consumption of

---

[6]Shirley Pettifer and Janet Torge, *A Book About Sexual Assault* (Montreal Press, 1987), p. 6.

alcohol or drugs. Since alcohol seems to play a significant role in dating in our society, this factor may be one that you can control more than any other factor.

Prevention Strategies

The most frequent victims of sexual assault are women between the ages of fourteen and nineteen years of age. The following prevention suggestions are useful for young people who are dating as well as for the more mature date. The acronym of DATE will be used for ease of recalling the suggestions for preventing a date rape.

*D*iagnose the risk factors for a date rape if you are even a little suspicious of the pending conditions. Chances are, if you sense that something may be wrong, it probably is. During diagnosis, discover as much information as possible about the potential date. The less information you have, the higher the potential risk. Who is this person? Where does he work? What do your friends know about his character? What do previous dates say about him? What is his reputation? What are his drinking or drug use habits? Where are you going? What time do you expect to return? How are you going there? What transportation alternatives do you have if you want to get away from your date?

These questions are representative of ones to ask yourself and others in order to assess some risk factors of an acquaintance assault. Of course, there is a chance that if you ask too many questions you might risk not getting the date. A balance must be found between healthy inquisitiveness and being paranoid. But diagnosis cannot occur unless you are aware that it is a necessary and a proper preventive step for you to take. Many victims of date rape agree. A recent U.S. Department of Justice Study, reported that "non-stranger rapes usually occurred in the victim's home (48%) or in or nearby a friend's home

(24%)."[7]

Diagnosis should not stop once the date begins. You will learn a lot about your date by asking some key questions of your date, covering any concerns you have. Remember that nonverbals can belie the spoken word. Look for inconsistencies and take note.

Abstinence from alcohol makes good sense for a number of health reasons. No or very limited alcohol consumption is a sound preventive measure. The potential victim who is intoxicated severely limits the self-defense options in case of a sexual assault. Severe intoxication will affect the memory of the victim to a degree that successful prosecution of the suspect may be hampered. Know your limits of consumption.

Be aware of the amount of alcohol that is being consumed by your date. Note any behavior changes in your date that are caused by alcohol consumption. You may be at risk as a passenger in your date's car for more than one reason if alcohol impairs physical and mental abilities. Assertion skills may be needed to communicate your concerns over the amount of alcohol that is being consumed. If you or your date are under the legal drinking age, your legal limits are zero. If you are of legal age, your alcohol limits are based on such factors as body size, metabolism, and food consumption.

Training and the development of good habits can be instrumental in preventing an acquaintance assault. Developing physical, verbal, and weapon alternatives as discussed earlier can enhance your options and chances of

---

[7]"Female Victims of Violent Crime," U.S. Department of Justice, Office of Justice Programs, Bureau of Justice Statistics, by Caroline Wolf Harlow, Ph.D., BJS Statistician, January, 1991, NCJ 126826, p. 12.

survival. Here are some additional suggestions for preventive habits to prevent date rapes:

1. Keep extra money available in case of emergencies. If you do not have the means of finding alternative ways home, like a taxi, you become somewhat dependant upon your date. If you choose to leave because of perceived threats to you, your options are somewhat expanded if you have your emergency fund available.

2. Keep a supply of dimes in case you need to make a phone call to summon assistance or arrange for transportation home. A phone credit card can also be a lifesaver as it removes the need to immediately pay for the local or long distance call.

3. Announce your agenda and itinerary to your friends and significant others. Announce to your date the time frames that you have in mind for the date. Be wary of any forceful suggestions to change the time frames you have announced.

4. Become familiar with physical techniques that may be useful in discouraging unwanted sexual advances. Assertive verbals are useful to communicate your wishes and concerns.

Expectations need to be communicated and understood by all parties, including parents. Parents should not hesitate to communicate their behavior expectations to the male half of the date. Parental expectations of their daughters should also be communicated. Reassurances, such as encouragement to call home immediately in case of any problems, lays out expectations clearly.

Women should not hesitate to assertively

communicate the "boundaries of interaction" to their date. Often a fear of potential rejection will create a reluctance to communicate emphatically when limits have been approached. Most of the vulnerability to date rape arises because people want to start off on the "right foot," make a good first impression, and not appear to be suspicious or paranoid.

Summary

It is natural not to expect danger while on a date or in similar social settings. It is easy to be lulled into a sense of complacency in such settings. Young people may be less aware of dangers because of ignorance of risks associated with acquaintance assaults. The statistics do tell a tale that should dictate care and caution when entering new relationships.

10. *Defense Strategies For Seniors*

*The key to preventing violent
crime against an older person is*

education.[1]

Senior citizens are more vulnerable to some crime risks. They are not immune from crimes such as sexual assault merely because of their advancing years. Senior citizens may be affected more by the fear of certain crimes than people from other age groups. The purpose of this chapter is to identify some crime risk areas for the senior citizen, and to offer crime prevention strategies to reduce these risks.

Changing Abilities

Every person possesses certain physical and mental strengths and weaknesses. These capabilities and limitations are determined by many factors such as physical handicaps, training and experience, ability to function under stressful situations, communication skills, and physical strength.

Our individual abilities and limitations are not static. They change commensurate with the aging process. Some examples include declining eyesight, hearing loss, reduced physical dexterity, and loss of strength. We must recognize changes in our physical abilities and seek to compensate when a deficiency is noted.

It is as important to recognize our limitations as it is to recognize our capabilities. Honest self-appraisal is necessary for self-improvement in defense skills. This self-appraisal begins with realizing the effects of aging on our ability for self-defense. Senior citizens need to "make up with the mind" what they may have "lost in their bodies." Be honest with yourself and realize what things you are no longer able to do, and then compensate.

---

[1]FBI Law Enforcement Bulletin, July 1988, Vol. 57 No. 7, "Violent Crime Against the Aging," p. 11, by Cynthia J. Lent and Joseph A. Harpoid.

Physical Changes

A central theme of this book has been to minimize the role that physical skills plays in self-defense and crime prevention. Good crime prevention habits are the key to minimizing the chances of becoming a victim of crime. Crime prevention habits can be learned at any age. Fatalistic attitudes about the inevitability of becoming a crime victim should not prevail merely because of diminishing physical abilities. Physical abilities do play a role in self-protection, but a relatively minor one.

The aging process begins to affect the body at about age forty. Some of the first signs of aging are a gradual loss of visual acuity, slowing reaction times, more "aches and pains" in muscle joints, and evident self-limitations in certain strenuous physical activities.

Some criminals will select older victims because they may feel less threatened while committing the crime. Some senior citizens may limit their "out of the home" activities because of a perceived inability to "protect themselves." The less a person participates in activities outside of the home, the more that fear could predominate.

Compensation Measures

1. **Prescriptions:** Know the effects that medical prescriptions have upon you. This is particularly true for new prescriptions and changed doses of existing prescriptions.

2. **Weather effects:** Cold or extremely hot weather will sap your strength. Be aware of the potential for climatic conditions to affect your physical abilities. Acclimate yourself to weather changes gradually, if possible.

3. **Sounds:** The sounds of the "outside world" can have a disconcerting effect upon your perceptive

abilities when first entered. Sounds can cause confusion and cause momentary disorientation.

4. **Walking:** Walk against traffic on a sidewalk. This position will give you an "oncoming" view of traffic. It should give added warning if a car were to swerve in your direction, or stop with the intention of grabbing your purse. When waiting at the curb to cross the street, give yourself a zone of safety from the edge of the curb. This provides a buffer should you lose your balance, or if a car should misjudge the curb while making a turn.

5. **Purse contents:** Do not burden yourself with extra "stuff" in your purse. These extras cause unnecessary weight resulting in unneeded fatigue. It also slows the process of finding keys and paying for purchases, and increases the chances of dropping important items. Make a photocopy of important papers such as your driver's license, social security card, and credit cards. Keep the copies at home for use if these items are ever lost or stolen.

6. **Carrying the purse:** The proper way to carry a purse is over the outside of the shoulder and held tightly to the side of your body. This position will limit the chance of being dragged or knocked down during a robbery by permitting you to easily release the purse. If the purse strap is wrapped around your wrist or neck you actually are tied to the purse and increase the chances of being knocked down or even dragged along the ground. If you do not have the strength to hold your purse properly and must routinely loop the shoulder strap around your neck in order to carry it, modify the purse strap to "break away" if grabbed harshly.

7. *Arriving at home:* Use additional exterior lighting at your home, particularly around exits and entrances. Consider the purchase and installation of a garage door opener which will limit your outside exposure to intruders and the climate. Technology exists to permit you to turn your lights on with remote control devices and to "alarm" your home to warn of intruders.

Swindles and Scams

There is no shortage of con artists and swindlers willing to take advantage of trusting and caring people. Con artists are normally very talented in their ability to persuade and convince others of their sincerity. These people are very persuasive and excellent actors. Generally the victims will be convinced that they will receive something for almost nothing, or services at a very reasonable price. In general, if it sounds too good to be true, it probably is.

Senior citizens are frequently the victims of shysters. This type of crime can have a tremendous emotional and financial impact due to limited earning power of seniors. These scams take many forms and usually involve the victim putting forth cash for home repairs, car repairs, a friend or relative, to help the "police" for a needy cause, and so on. A review of common types of scams may help protect you from becoming a victim:

1. *The "pigeon drop":* In a pigeon drop you might be approached by a person who claims to be from out of town. The person will appear to you to be very friendly, sweet, and caring. This person could be of any age, sex, or race, but commonly is a young female. The initial contact could be at any place, but will commonly be in a public place. This person may tell you about recently moving to the area and having recently received a large sum of money from an inheritance or other "legitimate" source.

If you are perceived to be receptive or a "good mark," you will soon be joined by another person. This second person may also pretend to be new to the area or "lost." The second person will have a package of some sort which he or she will claim to be delivering. The package may have a fictitious address on it. During the ensuing conversation, one of the two persons (remember, they are a team) will suggest that the package be opened. You will find what appears to be a large amount of money in the package and will be convinced by the pair that all three of you should "share" in this windfall.

A third person may now enter the picture. This new person may be a man who is to "hold" the found money for any one of a number of reasons. You will be asked to put up "good faith" money in order to collect your share of the found money. Your money must be shown to the third person who will then return your money plus your share of the found money. You will receive a package that is supposed to contain your money plus the found money.

As you might have guessed, the package you are given contains cut-up paper and the three con artists are on their way out of town. These criminals have a way of vanishing into thin air. Many victims will not report the crime because of embarrassment for being so trusting.

2. *The Bank Examiner:* In this scheme you will be contacted by phone by a person who claims to be a "bank examiner" or an officer from the bank. This "examiner" will tell of conducting an investigation into the accuracy of your bank account. You will be asked for information about your account including your account numbers, address, account amounts,

and so on. The person says he will call you back after the computer information is checked against your "facts." The same person will call you back in a few minutes and tell you that the computer really was not incorrect, but that one of the tellers from the bank has been stealing from your accounts.

The "bank examiner" will appeal to your sense of responsibility to the community and law enforcement and ask for you to "help catch" this dishonest teller. You will be asked to go to the bank to withdraw money from your account. After you withdraw your money you will be asked to give it to the examiner so it can be used as evidence to catch the dishonest teller.

You will be asked not to tell anyone, not even the local police, about this. Of course, the "agents" and "examiners" are really crooks. Once you turn your money over to them you will not see it again.

3. *Impersonators:* People may call you or appear at your door representing themselves as officials of various agencies. You could become a victim when called by a person who pretended to be a grandson or daughter and was in need of money. The money would be for some emergency. The caller might even know personal information about your family. Of course, the caller (your relative) would send a friend over to pick up the money. Someone then will appear at your door to take the money. Your money is gone and so is the con artist.

People might appear at your door and pretend to be police officers, utility company workers, a motorist who is out of gas, or from a charity. These people will try to enter your house, and once inside of your home, they will steal whatever they can. Often, more than one person will appear. While you are distracted in one place, the other person is stealing from other rooms. You may not see the second person -- they may enter your home through another door while you talk to the con artist at the front door. The person at the front door may merely ask for a drink of water, or to use the phone to call a wrecker.

4. **Home repairs scam**: You will be approached at your home by persons, usually two, who are driving a truck that has "construction" type equipment on it. The people will claim to be working on a large commercial construction project in the area and have "extra" materials. You will be offered a very appealing price for home repairs such as asphalt driveway sealing, metal roof-coating, plumbing, or lawn work. The work will be performed quickly and with inferior materials.

One common job performed is driveway sealing. The main ingredient will be gasoline which turns the asphalt driveway black and looks very nice until it rains! You will end up paying large amounts of money for virtually nothing.

5. **Free Inspections:** Some con artists will offer free furnace inspections and then "arrange" to make repairs of your furnace. These repairs will often be unnecessary and costly. If there is time, a second opinion from a local and reputable firm may confirm or deny the need for the repairs.

Tips to Prevent Fraud

A number of precautions can be taken to limit the opportunity for someone to involve you in one of these scams or swindles. The main theme of these suggestions is that you know with whom you are dealing. Deal with local and reputable companies and remember that there is no hurry. Take your time. Be suspicious of people who call you and appear at your door, or approach you in a public place. Call your local Department on Aging or the Better Business Bureau if you are at all suspicious. Other tips:

1. Never give personal or financial information over the phone. It is no one else's business what your account numbers are, how much money you have, when you come and go, and so on. Ask the person to communicate with you in writing in order to verify (somewhat) that they are from a reputable company. Police agencies or banks will not ask you to help them catch a dishonest teller.

2. Be wary of anyone who approaches you and claims to have found a large amount of money. This could be the prelude to a pigeon drop or other scam. Most cities have ordinances that prescribe how unclaimed money is returned to the finder. Suggest that you go to the police with the money and you will soon discover if the person is a con artist.

3. Do not withdraw your money from the bank or savings account to demonstrate your "good faith" to a stranger. Ask the advice of a trusted friend or local police agency if in doubt.

4. Be very cautious of people who ask to do repairs on your home with "extra" materials, or at extremely low prices. It is good business to secure several estimates from local companies before approving any repairs. If such people do appear at your door, obtain a complete description of the people and the vehicle (including the license number) and report it immediately to the police.

5. Never let anyone into your home unless you are absolutely sure that you know who they are and

why they are there. Most utility companies will call and schedule repairs. Police officers will fully identify themselves when asked. Confirmation calls to the agency are a method of verifying the identity and purpose of the visit. If in doubt, call a neighbor or friend to be present while these people are in your home. This can be a preventive step against sexual assault also.

6.   Be wary of people who call and pretend to be from the government with "rebates" from your Social Security check. The person may show up to pay you, and not have the correct change. You will inadvertently lead them to your money.

7.   Leave "bait" money in a fairly conspicuous place in your bedroom. This money will be a nominal amount and may satisfy the burglar so that he doesn't continue the search to find the "real" money.

8.   Stamp or mark the back of your checks "for deposit only" to prevent them from being cashed if stolen.

Remember -- a little mistrust on your part is healthy. Be a bit of a detective. Good detectives are suspicious and inquisitive. The case you solve may be your own.

Review and Conclusions

The challenge now is to be your own risk manager. The challenge is to actively develop a wholistic approach to crime prevention by adopting healthy crime prevention attitudes and daily practicing prevention behaviors.

> "Never leave to chance what
> can be achieved by
> calculation." -- Disraeli

The act of minimizing vulnerability is a calculated

effort by a responsible person seeking not to leave personal safety to chance. A risk manager investigates preventive techniques and strategies and applies them to daily routine. It is essential that you routinely practice "what if" scenarios and investigate practical alternatives for realistic application of physical, non-physical, and weapon alternatives. Make an investment in prevention techniques for personal and property protection by joining or starting a Neighborhood Watch Program in your neighborhood in conjunction with your police department.

> "I look upon indolences as a sort of suicide." -- Lord Chesterfield

A personal risk manager also recognizes attitudes that are apathetic toward practice and involvement in crime prevention techniques. A personal risk manager knows that the unrealistic belief that "It won't happen to me" is unsafe. To modify Lord Chesterfield's quote, *we look upon indolences (avoiding preventive exertion) as a sort of suicide (creating vulnerability)*.

Become informed and aware of crime prevention programs sponsored by your local law enforcement agency. Recognize that crime occurs when a criminal perceives an opportunity. Recognize it is your individual responsibility to learn and practice crime prevention techniques. Recognize your personal physical and emotional limitations and abilities and build upon them.

> "Unforeseen, they say, is unprepared." -- Dryden

An important component of personal risk management is honest appraisal and evaluation of your personal habits that may increase vulnerability to crime. Who is better qualified and informed to analyze the weaknesses, for example, in your home security? Who best knows which locks, doors, and windows have weaknesses and are points of vulnerability? Who best knows the routine and habits practiced by family members that lend opportunity to becoming a crime victim?

Evaluating and appraising personal safety habits need continuous review and reinforcement. Survey your home for security deficiencies. Check with your local law enforcement agency for a security survey. Discuss crime prevention issues with your family, friends and co-workers to discover their level of preparation for crime prevention. Eliminate known crime risks whenever possible.

> "But man's capacities have
> never been measured; nor are
> we to judge of what he can do
> by any precedents, so little has
> been tried." -- Thoreau

So little has been attempted in the arena of crime prevention and personal risk management. All people are victims of crime both directly and indirectly. We pay a high price for crime in terms of human life, suffering, fear, and financial loss. The question becomes, how much victimization is acceptable to you, your friends and family? Victims cannot control the choices made by the criminal, but do control many significant factors that affect the outcome of any given encounter with a criminal.

> "The more you know, the more
> you can save yourself and that
> which belongs to you, and do
> more work with less effort."
> -- Charles Kingsley

You have taken the first step to educate yourself. We hope this book has provided the framework upon which you will build additional knowledge about preventive strategies against crime. And assume responsibility to educate others about crime prevention. Law enforcement cannot do it alone.

> "A lost battle is a battle one believes lost." -- Marshall Ferdinand Foch

In many ways, a negative thinking person believes the battle regarding crime and its prevention is a lost battle. This attitude is neither accurate nor productive. To feel frustrated, angered, and disappointed about crime frequency in your community is normal. But these feelings should not defeat you, but rather arouse you to action.

Many people relinquish responsibility for crime prevention by believing it is only the job of law enforcement organizations to prevent crime. This apathetic attitude further aggravates the problem, and prevents them from taking preventive actions to combat the crime problem. Avoid this negative attitude by personally accepting responsibility to halt crime in your environment.

> "The concept of successful business merely consists of doing things in a very simple way, doing them regularly, and never neglecting to do them." -- Lord Leverhulme

Personal risk management is the important business of studying and practicing simple crime prevention techniques. You must practice them regularly, and never neglect to do them. This paraphrasing of Lord Leverhulme's quote holds the key to becoming a successful personal risk manager: Regular practice of simple (and not so simple) preventive techniques will result in self-defense habits, which will require little effort to continue.

The catch-phrase in the above quotation is, "never neglecting to do them." Preventive techniques require regular practice and thought. Most good things do.

Being your own risk manager is an attitude that becomes part of your life-style. Many people become motivated to learn and practice preventive techniques, for example, when a community is being terrorized by a rapist. But once the rapist is arrested or stops his assaults, a collective "sigh of relief" is heard, and the motivation for learning about crime prevention is soon abandoned.

Don't stop learning about crime prevention strategies. Practice what you have learned, and learn what you have practiced. This is the best defense strategy for women, and also for men. Do this, and you will indeed be your own risk manager.